JOHANN SEBASTIAN BACH

"Gentlemen, great news! The elder Bach has come."

Life Stories for Young People

JOHANN SEBASTIAN BACH

Translated from the German of

Ludwig Ziemssen

by

George P. Upton

YESTERDAY'S CLASSICS
ITHACA, NEW YORK

This edition, first published in 2024 by Yesterday's Classics, an imprint of Yesterday's Classics, LLC, is an unabridged republication of the text originally published by A. C. McClurg & Co. in 1905. For the complete listing of the books that are published by Yesterday's Classics, please visit www.yesterdaysclassics.com. Yesterday's Classics is the publishing arm of Gateway to the Classics which presents the complete text of hundreds of classic books for children at www.gatewaytotheclassics.com.

ISBN: 978-1-59915-493-0

Yesterday's Classics, LLC
PO Box 339
Ithaca, NY 14851

CONTENTS

Translator's Preface

THERE is no person in musical or general history whose life can be studied by young people with more advantage, or followed in its general characteristics with more profit than Johann Sebastian Bach. The old saying that genius is only the highest capacity for work has sometimes been attributed to him. Whether he originated the saying or not, his life illustrates its truth. His industry was astonishing, whether in adverse or prosperous circumstances, though his remuneration, considering the magnitude of his achievements, now seems a beggarly pittance. He worked for the highest in his art, and always with the utmost of his ability, and consecrated his work to the divine honor. Upon all his important pieces he inscribed the letters, "S. D. G." ("Soli Deo Gloria"), "to the glory of God alone." What the simple, God-fearing, art-loving cantor of Saint Thomas accomplished, the world knows. Gounod summed it up in the declaration that if all the music written since Bach's time were lost, it could be reconstructed upon what he wrote. His life was as noble as his music. He was an affectionate father, laboring manfully and incessantly to support his large family; a good citizen, faithfully fulfilling his duties and commanding universal respect; a musician without an equal in the profundity of his knowledge and the richness of his productions; the founder of modern music, the master of the organ, the composer of the highest forms of sacred music; a plain, humble man, despising rank and show, making no boast of his grand achievements, and yet recognized in the court of Frederick the Great as above courtiers and nobility by the title of his genius. "Seest thou a man diligent in business; he shall stand before kings." He was a self-reliant, self-sustained, evenly poised man, plain and unostentatious in his bearing, honorable in his intercourse with men, strong and unvarying in his home love, and guided in every event of life by a strict morality born of sincere religion. He followed the bent of his genius untrammelled by the accidents or troubles of life, and sought for no higher reward than his own conviction of the worth of his accomplishments. Such a life is to be commended not only to the young student entering upon the profession of music, but to every young person entering upon the duties of life. This little volume, therefore, worthily claims a place among "Life Stories for Young People." Though the original is inaccurate in some small details, which later biographers have corrected, the general story of his life is reliable and nearly every event of importance is included in its pages.

G. P. U.

CHICAGO, 1905

CHAPTER I

A FRIEND IN NEED

AT the close of a beautiful Summer day, in the year 1699, subdued and solemn strains of music from the little house of the organist of the market-town of Ohrdruff[1] floated through its quiet streets. A boy sat crying upon the stone steps leading to the house-door. Now and then he lifted his head, looked into the hallway, and saying in a mournfully complaining tone, "False again," or, "The second violin plays most abominably," or making some similar protest of musical sensibility, bowed his head again in sorrow and tears.

As he sat thus, a quick step was heard coming up the street. A lad, somewhat older than the other, approached and said in a clear, cheerful voice: "Why are you crying, Bastian, and what means this funeral music?"

The one addressed raised his handsome eyes, red with weeping, bowed in a dejected manner to

[1]Ohrdruff is a little manufacturing town in Saxe-Coburg-Gotha, about eight miles south of Gotha.

1

his questioner, and said in a low voice: "My brother is dead. Did you not know it?"[2]

"I had not heard a word of it," he replied. "All last week I was at my cousin's in Eisenach,[3] and I have but just returned. Is he dead? And so suddenly! Poor boy, I pity you from my heart. When did it happen?"

"Last evening just about this time. He had not been in his usual health for a week. He often complained of dizziness and difficulty in breathing, and yesterday while cleaning his old violin he suddenly fell and died."

Passionate sobs made his last words almost unintelligible, and the boy for a few seconds gave way to irrepressible grief.

His young friend regarded him in silence for a time, and when he had somewhat recovered from his passionate sobbing delicately sought to divert his attention from his troubles by asking, "Who are these playing so wretchedly? Friends of the deceased?"

"Three of them are. They have engaged the town clerk's assistant for second violin, and he plays badly enough to set one's teeth on edge. If my dead brother

[2] After the death of his father and mother, Sebastian Bach was adopted by his elder brother, Johann Christoph, the organist and music master at Ohrdruff, who gave him his earliest lessons in singing and piano-playing.

[3] Eisenach, a little town in Thuringia, was the birthplace of Sebastian Bach. It is also famous for the Wartburg, which stands on one of the hills near the town, where Luther lived at one time and translated the Bible into German, and as being the scene of many of the song contests of the Minnesingers.

could hear him, he would jump out of his coffin and drive the bungler out of his house."

His friend smilingly nodded assent. "He is certainly a slovenly player, but it can't be helped now."

"That is true," sobbed the boy.

A brief pause in the conversation was filled with the tones of the funeral music, during which his friend's gaze rested thoughtfully and sympathetically upon the countenance of his mournful comrade, and his lips moved as if he were talking to himself. At last he resumed reluctantly, but with manifest cordiality and good-will: "Well, Bastian, what is to be done now that your brother, the organist, is dead?"

"The town will install a new organist, I suppose."

"Of course, but that is of little consequence; I mean what will become of you?"

"Of me?" replied Sebastian, thoughtfully. "Who can say? But with God's help I will become a skilful musician, like my good father, and as all the Bachs have been for a hundred years past."

"You mistake my question," said his friend. "I mean where will you live now that this house is henceforth to be closed? You are now a poor orphan. Do you expect that any of your relatives will take you in?"

Sebastian shook his head. "No, Erdmann,[4] I do not. Who can do it? My only remaining brother, Johann

[4] George Erdmann was a schoolfellow of Sebastian Bach and an excellent musician, though in after life he followed other pursuits.

Jakob, has left the country and gone into business in Sweden. Both my uncles, my father's brothers, have been dead for some years, and my cousins have trouble enough to get along upon their small chorister's allowance without being burdened with me. Again—"

"It must be very hard for you, my poor Bastian."

Sebastian for a moment regarded his sympathetic friend with moistened eyes, then cordially took his arm and went slowly down the street with him.

"I will tell you about this, Erdmann; they possibly may look at the matter differently. The relatives will come to the funeral ceremonies in the morning, and it may be perhaps that this or that one will take me in until something definite can be arranged; but I am not sure that I wish them to do so. How could I be happy? These poor people have no higher ambition than to get musical education enough to fit them for an ordinary organist's position and enable them to secure a place in some Thuringian country town, and, when they get it, to go on, day after day, practising noble music as if it were a trade, just as if they were cobblers or tailors. If I were to find a home with cousins Tobias Friedrich, Johann Bernhard, Johann Christoph, or Johann Heinrich, what would become of me? All my life I should hear only the music I made myself. I should make no progress, I should never penetrate the noble mysteries of our art; I should remain a town musician like a thousand others."

"But, Bastian, why should you trouble yourself about these matters? Why fix a goal for yourself now? You are still very young."

"I am old enough to know that I must escape from this narrow musical life. Even if my brother had lived, I should not have remained with him much longer."

"Why not? He was a skilful musician."

"Yes, but only for himself. He either could not or would not assist me to advance. I was disgusted with his dry and uninteresting exercises, and he refused to let me practise more useful and difficult ones. He had a manuscript volume of piano studies by famous masters, like Froberger, Fischer, Kerl, Pachelbel, Buxtehude, Bruhns, and Böhm—valuable works, I assure you. Do you suppose he allowed me to have them? When I begged for the volume, he refused me and locked it up."

"This is strange. Why should he have acted so? He could not possibly keep you from advancing in the art for which you have such decided talent."

"Certainly not. He could do well for himself, like all the old organists round here, but he had not the faculty of making others progress. There is something forbidding and mysterious in the attitude of these old musicians of this stamp, which makes it very difficult for beginners to acquire even the rudiments."

"That is curious; but did you at last secure those beautiful and difficult musical exercises?"

An arch smile lit up Sebastian's countenance, immediately followed by an indignant expression: "It is a sad story, Erdmann, and it makes me feel angry whenever I think of it. But listen. My brother had locked up the manuscript in a cabinet which did not shut very closely. I determined to get it, for otherwise I should remain an ignorant scholar and make no advance. One night, when my brother was asleep, I squeezed my hands—they are so little—between the wires of the cabinet and pulled the roll out, not, however, without rubbing the skin off my hands pretty badly, and carried my treasure safely away to my little chamber, where, as I had no candle, I copied the whole book by moonlight."

"Why, you little sinner," said Erdmann, laughing and amazed, "I call that perseverance. How long did it take you to copy it?"

"Fully six months, and my eyes are weak in consequence. And after this what do you suppose happened? One day my brother came in, unawares, when I had the exercises, and without saying by your leave carried off my precious treasure. He never brought it back, notwithstanding all my tearful entreaties."

"Dreadful!" exclaimed Erdmann. "Worse than dreadful! How could he do it? I should have hated him."

"No! He is still my brother. He has done me many kindnesses, and I am greatly distressed," his voice trembled again, "greatly distressed at his death, and just as he was cleaning the old violin! He believed it was a genuine Amati and insisted that Antonio Amati's name and symbols were pasted on it in my grandfather's time, but I do not believe it. The tone is much too hard and rasping. I think it is an old Tyrolean country violin."[5]

[5] The Amatis were a world-renowned family of violin-makers living at Cremona, Italy, in the sixteenth and seventeenth centuries. The most famous members of the family were Andrea A., died in 1577, the maker of the first violin; Nicola, =>

"So? Will he be buried to-morrow?"

"Yes."

"And then your fate must be decided?"

"Certainly it must. The cousins then must give me my copy of the book."

"They ought to do that at least. But tell me, what else must they give you?"

"I shall only claim what belongs to me. On an upper shelf in the cabinet there is a tin box with my christening-money, two medals inherited from my great-uncle, Heinrich, and a little money left me by my good father, which they must give me, must they not, Erdmann?"

"I suppose so. You are certainly very young yet, Bastian."

"Young!" replied the latter, indignantly. "I am thirteen—almost fourteen years old. It is high time I was learning something useful, hearing good music, becoming acquainted with great compositions, and I cannot do that here or elsewhere in Thuringia. I must go to some great city where the musical life is intense, where famous organists delight congregations on Sunday, and public libraries lend their best books. It is for such reasons as these I cannot stay with my cousins, even if they should cordially invite me. Now, do you understand, Erdmann?"

1568-1586; Antonio, 1589-1627; and Nicolo, 1596-1684, that last of the great violin-makers of the family.

During this statement his friend had been thoughtfully regarding the little Sebastian—he was very small for his age—and at last tenderly said: "I believe you are right, Sebastian. Were you to remain here you would be in wretched circumstances like all the other Bachs, although they have musical talent by nature. You must get away, and I will make you this proposition: Day after to-morrow I am going to see my mother's brother at Lüneburg.[6] Go with me. Lüneburg is not a great city, but it is a much more important place than Ohrdruff, Arnstadt, or Eisenach. It was for long the residence of the Grand Duke of Brunswick, and it still has many of the advantages of a capital. There is a magnificent organ in the old Gothic Church of St. John, and every Sunday you can hear the best of music there. You would enjoy that, I fancy."

Sebastian stood for a moment with glistening eyes, overcome with joy. "Lüneburg!" he replied with trembling voice, "St. John's Church organ! Oh, Erdmann, the great organist Böhm,[7] whose majestic chorales I copied by moonlight, is the leading player there. Oh, to hear him, to hear him, I would go barefoot to Lüneburg!"

"Yes," said Erdmann, pleased with the acceptance of his proposal, "that will be nice for you, and a few miles from there is Hamburg."

---

[6] The capital of Lüneburg in the province of Hanover, Prussia.

[7] George Böhm, a countryman of Bach, was born at Goldbach in 1661. He was one of the greatest organists of his time.

"Where the famous Reinken, Johann Adam Reinken,[8] plays splendidly at St. Katherine's Church," interposed Sebastian, with enthusiasm. "Erdmann, my dear Erdmann, I must go; and if you will take me with you I will thank you all my life long."

"If your relatives consent, I shall not fail to do so," said his friend. "And once you are in Lüneburg, my uncle, if I ask him, will gladly help you to go farther."

"Really?" said Sebastian, overcome with delight. "Oh, dear friend, how fortunate I am to have met you! I am determined to go with you whether my cousins consent or not."

His more considerate friend advised him to keep on good terms with his relatives. "I will come in the morning and inquire," said he. "Only be very judicious, so that they may have confidence in your good judgment and give their consent to your plans."

"Yes, I will. But come, be sure to come," implored Sebastian, in a beseeching tone, as he pressed his friend's hand. "And not too late. The funeral takes place immediately after the noon service, and promptly afterward everything necessary must be done, for most of the guests will wish to leave before evening, so that they may be punctual at their posts on Monday morning. There will not be much time to spare."

---

[8]Reinken was born at Deventer in 1663 and died as organist of St. Katherine's Church, in Hamburg, in 1722. He had remarkable talent both as player and composer and was greatly esteemed by Bach.

"You are right. The procession passes our house and I can then fix the time. Leave it all to me."

"Yes, I will do so, dear Erdmann, and already I give you a thousand thanks. It seems as if a new life were opening for me. Oh! Oh! to hear Böhm play, and perhaps even Reinken, and to hear their works and play them! Could anything be finer?"

"Well," replied his friend, endeavoring to moderate his enthusiasm, "the world has much besides this that is worth living for. But it is nice that you are pleased with your prospects. Doing things by halves will not accomplish much of any value."

"That shall never be said of me," interposed Sebastian, with flashing eyes. "I feel that I can accomplish something of value, but I must do it in the right way and in the right place—in Lüneburg. Lüneburg is now my watchword. I shall not shut my eyes this night. Would it were morning!"

"Have patience. The morning will not fail you. So now, *auf wiedersehen*."

"I can scarcely wait."

"But you must. Good-bye."

"Good-bye. I will hurry home to pack my things."

Thus the friends separated in the twilight, in the narrow streets of Ohrdruff.

CHAPTER II

IN THE WORLD

THE funeral of the organist and music master, Johann Christoph Bach, was marked by all the ceremony becoming the burial of an excellent man, a faithful servant of the church and school, and an accomplished musician. The mourners returned from the churchyard, speaking with subdued voices. They were plain, earnest men, clad in simple black coats, long-skirted waistcoats over short knee-breeches and stockings, and buckled shoes. They also wore the three-pointed hat over a small periwig.

Arrived at the house, those not belonging to the family took their departure after a few words of condolence, but the relatives entered and assembled in the sitting-room of the deceased around the old black family-table, which had been made ready for such business as it might be necessary for them to settle before they separated. This did not take long. The joint bequest, very moderate in amount, fell to the five sons of the deceased, to be divided at a fitting time. The principal difficulty was to decide as to the further care and education of the little Johann Sebastian; but they were spared any trouble on his account, for they had hardly begun to consider the question when Sebastian, who had been sitting in the window looking at the funeral hymn, arose, and decorously advanced to the table.

"Dear cousins," he boldly began, looking round the circle with large, bright eyes, "do not trouble yourselves about me. I am in my fourteenth year and am old enough to take care of myself hereafter. I thank my dead brother for all the love and kindness which he bestowed upon me to the very end, but I am not willing longer to be a burden to anyone; I shall leave this good home as early as possible to-morrow to seek my fortunes elsewhere. I beg you to give me the organ compositions which Johann Christoph took away from me, likewise the old box with my christening-money, together with your blessing, and let me go in peace."

All present were greatly astonished at the boy's bold little speech, and there was silence in the room for a time. It was broken by the most prominent one in the circle, Johann Valentin, eldest son of George Christoph, cantor at Schweinfurt, who said: "Your statement greatly astonishes us, dear Johann Sebastian; you are not yet of age nor able to earn a living by the practice of our beloved music. Tell us what your plans are and how you expect to support yourself. Your little christening-money will not go far."

"My first move will be to the city of Lüneburg," said the boy, with confidence, "where I hope to take lessons from the great organist, Böhm. My friend Erdmann, who has a kind uncle living there, goes to him to-morrow, and will take me with him and introduce me to him. I have a good singing voice and an excellent method, so I expect I shall easily secure a position as chorister and thus provide for the ordinary expenses of life. In case of extreme need, my friend Erdmann has promised me his uncle's assistance."

Johann Valentin replied: "Our family, honorably known as the Bachs, are of a contented spirit by nature, and have always been so well satisfied with their fatherland and their circumstances that, with the exception of your brother, Johann Jakob, none of them until now has desired to seek service and fortune outside of Thuringia. The Bachs until now have considered the approbation of their superiors and of their native places as more desirable than the quest for fame at great trouble and expense among jealous strangers. Are you now to be an exception, dear Johann Sebastian? Do you not believe one can become a good organist here, one well pleasing to God and man, and live here contented with his position? Your good father, Johann Ambrosius, I think, set you a commendable example. How is it then that you alone have this restlessness and this inordinate desire to associate with so-called 'great musicians'? Oh, my dear Johann Sebastian, music is not a mere matter of show and glory; it is a solemn reality. It is of little consequence whether the world hears of us, so that we strive with all our might that God may hear us and recognize our simple art."

"What you say, cousin," replied Sebastian, with an earnestness not often found in one so young, "is as true as gold, and yet I cannot longer remain satisfied with what our family has thus far accomplished. What I mean is, that the Bachs should not continuously learn only from the Bachs. They must go out into the world. Every master craftsman lets his son go among strangers so that he may learn some other master's style and ways, and thus improve, or, as it were, bring fresh blood into his workmanship. Painters and sculptors go to Italy, where there are good masters and teachers, and infuse new life into their artistic work at home; while musicians alone sit immovable in their little organ-lofts and hear no one but themselves. There is no progress in that. And it is because I believe all this that I am determined to travel and try to study in other places and among other people, to hear good musicians, and to learn from them what I need to learn."

The boy's eyes glistened and his cheeks reddened as he spoke. He grew more and more excited as he proceeded, until at last he was well-nigh breathless. Finally, he ceased and looked around the circle, awaiting a gracious answer. But the cousins were also silent, and looked at each other as if paralyzed by the boy's passionate utterances, until at last Johann Ernst, Johann Christoph's eldest son, expressed the sentiment of the family, and said, in a tone of the deepest conviction, "It is only pride and the craving for empty honors that have induced you to leave here."

"That is not so," replied Sebastian, excitedly. "I am striving for the same ends as you, only in my own way.

If I master my art, I will elevate and improve sacred music in a worthy and judicious manner; I will play for the praise of the Lord. I will walk honestly, as did my blessed father. If I seek other ends than these may someone shatter my instrument, for I shall no longer be worthy to touch the consecrated keys."

It was no longer a boy who spoke, but a young man, who had seriously considered his art and who was determined nothing should turn him from the right way to the highest achievements.

As such a youth the Bachs at last recognized him. After a whispered consultation the eldest voiced the final decision: "We have agreed, dear Johann Sebastian, to let you go the way you have chosen, hoping and praying it may end well; we have the utmost confidence in the sincerity of your purpose, and as for the rest we leave you in the Almighty's hands. Forget not, among strangers, who you are and where you belong. We, the elders, will remain here, and when you return to the dear Thuringian land, come as a true Bach, as an able and pious musician, as a worthy son of your brave, faithful father."

"I promise you all solemnly to do so," said Sebastian, with deep emotion, as he extended his hand to each cousin, beginning with Valentin. They shook it warmly and firmly, as a mark of conciliation, and then Johann Valentin took a gulden from his little purse, as did all the others, and handed the modest sum to the blushing boy as his travel-money. They also gave him the tin savings-box with the christening-money, and beside this his well-earned manuscript, an autograph motet[9] of his dead brother's ("Lord, if I have only Thee") for five voices, with the fundamental bass, and finally added to his brother's bequest a violin (not the supposed Amati), as well as the bow and case, so that the little traveller "may have the opportunity further to perfect himself on this instrument."

Then they dismissed the boy, who was overcome with joy and gratitude, to give him time to make his simple plans for the journey. He rushed out as if beside himself with happiness, which was still further intensified by the appearance of his true friend Erdmann at the door, whom he embraced without any regard to the parcels in his arms.

"Erdmann, dearest Erdmann," he shouted, scarcely lowering his voice, "I am free! I am going with you, God be praised!"

"Have they really let you go, and with their free consent?" said the astonished Erdmann.

"With their free consent," replied Sebastian. "At first they hesitated. They thought it improper for a Bach to go among strangers and to wish to study with other masters, but I argued so stoutly against that view, and defended my plans so earnestly, that at last they trusted me and gave their consent with many good wishes. They also contributed an ample sum of travel-money, and

---

[9]The term 'motet' is applied to church music set to Biblical texts for several voices, of moderate length, and without instrumental accompaniment.

gave me this violin and a composition as a remembrance of my dead brother,—but, oh, I could have remembered him without that." And the great spiritual eyes of the boy glistened with rising emotion.

"Now all goes well," said Erdmann. "Your cousins have taken the right view of the case. You are free, and nothing can prevent you from becoming a great musician—greater than all the Bachs, big and little, before you."

"Yes, yes," cried Sebastian, trembling with joy; "but when shall we start?"

"The first thing in the morning. We have a good conveyance to Gotha and day after to-morrow to Mühlhausen. Bring your baggage this evening to the Black Bear and be there yourself to-morrow morning at sunrise."

"Hurrah!" shouted Sebastian, excitedly. His outcry rang so loudly through the house that one of the Bach cousins opened the door and reproved him: "Johann Sebastian, we are still in the house of death."

"Forgive me," said the really contrite lad, turning crimson, as he started up to his little chamber, while Erdmann, taking some of the reproof to himself, quietly withdrew.

Thus the memorable day came to an end crowning Sebastian's dearest wishes. His joy could hardly have been greater had he been vouchsafed a glance into the future and realized he was taking the first step upon the road leading him to the supreme heights of his art.

With eager hands he joyfully packed the little bag left him by his devoted father with his scanty stock of clothes and the necessary books and papers, and took it in the darkness of the evening to the Black Bear, where the old and well-known house-servant took care of it. Then he hastened back to the organist's house, bade a cordial farewell to his relatives, ate a little soup in the kitchen, made for him by the old housemaid, took a big slice of bread, and hurried up to his chamber so that he might have a good night's rest and be ready for his early start.

There was not much sleep for him, however, that night. He lay upon his bed with wide-open eyes looking out into the serene moonlight. Like the light clouds which floated across the moon, memories and hopes swept over his young soul. Gentle, beautiful melodies entranced him and made his heart beat exultantly. Half waking, half dreaming, he raised his hands as though they touched the keys of a celestial instrument and his lips murmured disconnected words.

Thus the night hours passed between waking and sleeping. Toward morning he sank into the deep, sound sleep of youth, and notwithstanding his longings and his impatience for the journey would have slept beyond the appointed hour had not his trusty friend, the old housemaid, awakened him and reminded him of his purpose, at the first glow of dawn. It was a joyful call. Thankfully he threw his arms about her neck and drew her old head down to his. Then he dismissed her, arose and dressed, bathed his flushed face in cold water, and repaired to the kitchen, where he sat by the maidservant a few minutes while he ate his morning soup.

At last he was through. He bade farewell to his tearful friend and was about to leave the house, when a room door opened and the plain, honest face of Johann Valentin appeared.

"Johann Sebastian."

"Dear cousin."

"Come in."

As the boy stood before him, he placed both hands upon his shoulders and looked into his clear blue eyes.

"My dear Johann Sebastian," he said with deep emotion, "my heart bids me say a word to you before you leave your home. Some voice clearly tells me that great achievements and fame are in store for you. But whatever may be the outcome of the course you take this day, contrary to the usages and habits of our family, the greatest human fame is as nothing in God's eyes if it is not humbly received by a pure and pious heart, which ascribes the honor to Him. Remember this, dear Johann Sebastian, and take from me, the eldest of the family, in place of your dear father, my heartiest wishes and blessings."

He placed his hand upon the boy's head, whispered a prayer, kissed him lightly upon the forehead, and softly said, "Now go in peace."

"You shall not be disappointed in me, dear cousin," said the boy with emotion, as he reverently kissed the hand of his well-wisher. "I shall never forget your words, never, and never shall I cease to be grateful for your fatherly kindness. Farewell."

"God's angels guide and guard you."

The next moment he had left the organist's house and with weeping eyes was hastening down the deserted street.

CHAPTER III

THE FIRST STEP TO FAME

"GOOD-MORNING! It is well that you are here at last, Sebastian," exclaimed Erdmann, as he advanced to meet his friend. "The horses are already harnessed in the yard and the driver has not had to wait long for you. Come in at once."

"Yes, yes," said the breathless boy; "is my bag put on?"

"Certainly. I took it to the wagon myself. What is that slung on your back?"

"My own violin. My cousins gave it to me as part of my brother's legacy. It was kind of them, don't you think so?"

"Yes, but now let us go in. The driver is taking his morning beer in the kitchen and we must make arrangements for our transportation."

The two friends hastened in, and introduced themselves to the honest Jehu, who received them with a grunt of recognition. Then the young passengers climbed into the wagon, a somewhat primitive style of vehicle with a canvas cover stretched over hoops, fixed a convenient place for themselves and their luggage among some sacks of hay in the back, and a few minutes later were rattling down the quiet street with happy hearts, thence out through the low, dark town-gate into the level country, which was most attractive in the early morning light. On every side the early-awakened birds were holding jubilant matin service in the bushes and trees.

It was a delightful journey, notwithstanding the rough country roads and the jolting wagon, for the young travellers were in excellent spirits. They rolled up the canvas cover and keenly enjoyed the fresh beauty of the summer morning. Every village they passed was a source of wonder, every cornfield a delight to their eyes, every wood an unsurpassed pleasure; with quick eyes they followed the flight of every bird, and with attentive ears they listened to every sound, nigh and far. They drank in the perfume of the clover with zest. They even enjoyed the bitter crab-apples, which they plucked as they passed, as if they had been sweet dainties.

But now and then more serious feelings rose in the hearts of the lads. As they were riding through a country village a funeral procession crossed their way, the mourners singing a chorale. Their joyous chatter ceased. Erdmann sorrowfully regarded the sad spectacle, but Sebastian took his violin from his case and played a beautiful accompaniment to the chorale.

They talked almost ceaselessly of their past and of the future, but the city of Lüneburg, the end of their journey, was the principal theme of conversation.

Erdmann, who had previously been in the old Hanse city, had to describe the place over and over before his young companion's questions were satisfied. Sebastian pictured it to himself as the greatest and most imposing city he had ever known, with ancient and beautifully decorated gabled buildings, great shops and warehouses, majestic churches and cloisters. As he listened to Erdmann's description he fancied himself sailing up and down the river, climbing the high Kalkberg to the St. Michael's School, wandering through the halls of the old Rathhaus, going down into the gypsum quarries near by, and wandering among the leafy recesses of the Göhrde.[10] In return for Erdmann's delightful story, Sebastian related the events of his early life at home and told of his father's masterly skill in organ and violin playing. The good-natured Erdmann listened to him with deep or at least apparently deep interest, and volunteered questions to bring out new information.

"It is certainly most extraordinary," said he, when an opportunity offered itself, "that a talent for the same art should have appeared without a break in one and the same family and in all its numerous branches. It has already come to this, that they call all skilful organists in Thuringia 'Bach,' without regard to their names, for all Bachs are skilful organists."

"That is so," replied Sebastian, "and my blessed father, Johann Ambrosius, was one of the most skilful of them all. He inherited this gift from his

---

[10]A large and beautiful forest, containing a hunting-castle, within the jurisdiction of Lüneburg.

great-grandfather, Veit Bach,[11] who left Hungary for Germany two centuries ago to enjoy religious liberty, for he was a faithful adherent of the Lutheran Church. He found this liberty in Thuringia, settled down in the village of Wechmar, near Gotha, where he opened its first bakery and practised music for his own pleasure. He had learned it from the gypsies, and played skilfully on the zither, a kind of lute."

"And this Veit Bach," said Erdmann, smiling, "has transmitted his talent through his numerous posterity to you?"

"That he has," said Sebastian, with emphasis. "His son Hans gave up the bakery and was apprenticed to the town-piper of Gotha. He lived at that time in the tall tower of the old guildhall and there Hans fiddled and piped in the jolliest way. It is said he was a 'hail-fellow-well-met,' and welcome everywhere. My father had a picture of him playing the violin, with a large bell on his left shoulder. Under it is written:

> "Here you see, fiddling, stands Hans Bach,
> To hear him play would make you laugh.
> He plays, you must know, in a way of his own,
> And wears a fine beard by which he is known."

Erdmann laughed loudly. "He must have been a queer fellow," said he. "He would have suited me."

[11] Veit Bach, the founder of the Bach family, was a baker at Presburg, on the Danube. After leaving Hungary he settled in Wechmar, Thuringia, and carried on his business there. He played the lute and, it is related, was so fond of it that he used to play it while his corn was being ground. His son, Hans, was the first of the Bachs to make music a profession.

"He ought to have suited anyone," said Sebastian. "His musical talent descended to his three sons. Johann was organist at the church in Erfurt, known as the 'Predige Church'; Christoph, my grandfather, died as a member of the Arnstadt town band; and Heinrich as town organist, also in Arnstadt. The family tendency was so strong in him, my father used to say, that even as a boy he would run miles to hear an organ played and to learn something. All three of these have composed some excellent music."

"It is remarkable," said Erdmann.

"Yes, and Johann as well as Heinrich had three sons. All six became musicians, and their children and grandchildren after them."

"Who would have believed it? It is astonishing! Now tell me about your good father."

"He was truly a distinguished musician. The people of Eisenach thoroughly appreciated their Court and town musician. His resemblance to his twin brother, Johann Christoph, was remarkable. My mother has often told me that she and her sister-in-law could not have told them apart when they were together but for their dress. They were also wonderfully alike in disposition, speech, gait, and sentiments. They were exactly similar in the style and execution of their music, also. When one of them was sick the other was, and they died almost at the same time. Is it not both beautiful and touching?"

"It is so. You Bachs are indeed a peculiar family.

Take care, Bastian, that you also prove a worthy member of it."

"Let us hope so. You may be sure I shall work hard for it."

Thus chatting with each other and enjoying the journey with all the zest and enthusiasm of youth, the lads reached Gotha, and after a quiet night's rest at a modest inn went on to Mühlhausen. Thence they continued their journey on foot, now and then getting a ride when anyone was kind enough to pick them up. Their luggage had been intrusted by the practical Erdmann to a business house which had relations with Lüneburg and undertook to forward it to his uncle's well-known house.

After seven days' travelling they reached Lüneburg fresh and happy, and were received by Erdmann's uncle with that cordial and friendly hospitality which his nephew had anticipated.

Sebastian quickly made a good impression upon the old gentleman, especially by his precocity and the intelligence which shone in his attractive eyes. The impression changed to one of respectful admiration when, a few days after their arrival, he seated himself at the old gentleman's fine Silbermann piano[12] and played

---

[12]The Silbermanns were a distinguished family of piano and organ makers whose instruments were highly prized in the seventeenth and eighteenth centuries. The most famous of this name was Gottfried (1683-1753), who lived at Freiburg. He built forty-two organs and introduced the present piano, then known as "hammer-clavier," into Germany. Bartolomeo Cristofori, who died in Florence in 1731, undoubtedly invented =>

his favorite chorale ("All is well, O Friend of my Soul"), which abounds in characteristic harmony, beautiful modulation, and rich melody. He promised to use his influence in getting him a position in the choir of the St. Michael's School, and he kept his word. On the very next day the stately old gentleman waited upon the Rector of the school, and stated the purpose of his visit so enthusiastically that the latter smilingly gave his assent and arranged with the leader of the choir that Johann Sebastian should have a trial of his voice in his presence.

The boy stood the test so well that the old choir-leader declared he was a most valuable acquisition. His voice was sonorous and of fine quality, strong and of good range, and beside this he read everything at sight and displayed such a remarkable knowledge of counterpoint that the Rector and leader were alike astonished. The former assigned him a room near his own and he was given a position as soprano singer, or discantist, in the choir as well as a seat at the free table[13] of the school. Sebastian's dearest wish was now gratified, and on the same day, after cordially thanking his benefactor, he settled down in the St. Michael's School, occupying a modest little room in a wing, with three other pleasant discantist companions.

Thenceforth he had to be industrious, very

---

this instrument and gave it its present name, pianoforte, but Silbermann greatly improved it.

[13]Certain scholars in the institution, known as "matin scholars," received free instruction as compensation for their singing in the choir.

industrious, for it was only by extraordinary effort that he could retain the advantage of the free position, and only by unusual industry that he could save time enough from school duties to gratify his musical inclinations. The St. Michael's School at that time had an abundance of the richest material, which was accessible to him. In a chapel at the side of the school there was a fine little organ, upon which he was occasionally allowed to play after he had demonstrated his ability to do so. There was also a rich collection of old musical manuscripts, in which he could revel to his heart's content whenever he had the time. Beside these, there were old and well-preserved instruments, violins, violas, violoncellos, lutes, etc. Had it only been permissible he would gladly have devoted his nights to the acquisition of the contents of these treasures, as he once had done in Ohrdruff; but nothing prevented his use of them in the daytime, and he was as happy as a king when he could lose himself in a flood of the old masters' harmonies.

Only one thing troubled him. He could not often improve and strengthen his organ-playing by listening to the great players. Ordinarily it was only possible to hear Böhm, the famous organist, on Sundays, and at such times Sebastian was confined to the church of the school by his duties as discantist, and other opportunities to hear him were so rare that there was little prospect of his gratifying his desire to listen to the master's richly flowing melodies, without making extra exertion. So he inquired of the sexton and organ-blower of St. John's Church when the great artist played on week days in the always closed church. Then, with the gracious connivance of the organ-blower, to whom he paid many a shilling out of his small store, he would slip into the church, ascend the tower into the loft, and there, resting upon his knees near an opening, would listen with trembling, delighted heart to the now lovely, again powerful, but always devout playing of the master. He paid careful attention to every nuance, to every peculiar method of tone production, and to the style of performance, so as to fix them in his memory. When the playing was over he would rush back to his room, take out the compositions of Böhm, which he had once copied with such infinite care and trouble, and pore over them as if the pieces which he had just heard had been brought to him by Böhm himself for performance.

He also cultivated violin-playing to the best of his ability, and with the help of his extraordinary natural gifts entered so deeply into the real nature of this simple yet marvellously expressive instrument that even with his still imperfect technic he produced the finest quality of tone, and when he extemporized seemed to be holding a dialogue with his own genius.

Many a time in the evening, when his roommates had sought their beds and all was silent in the large halls, he would spend hours in the moonlight, walking up and down the little room, lightly using his bow, and softly singing the second part to the melody he was playing, greatly to the delight and astonishment of the boys, while he himself was as happy as if he were living in a higher and serener sphere.

About this time a peculiar change took place in his

beautiful voice. As he was singing one day in the choir, he heard himself involuntarily singing as it were with a double voice—in soprano and in a lower octave— to the great surprise of the leader and not less to his own consternation. His consternation increased when he realized during the next few weeks that he could neither speak nor sing except in octaves, and bitter was his sorrow when he found that this condition, instead of disappearing, speedily grew worse, and that his beautiful voice was gone forever. He wept piteously and moaned: "Alas! now I can only be half a musician through life, for my highest and noblest instrument is ruined and can never be replaced."

Beside his grief over the loss of this beautiful divine gift, he was now troubled with painful solicitude as to his immediate future. It was solely on account of his accomplishments as a discantist in the choir that he had enjoyed the great privilege of the free position in the school. What would happen were this to be taken away from him? What would become of his musical and general education? Utter despair overcame his strong, vigorous spirit. "What will become of me? What will become of me?" he bitterly ejaculated. His pale, anxious face showed his severe troubles.

One day the Rector of the school unexpectedly summoned him, and to his great delight and surprise informed him that, owing to the loss of his singing-voice, he would be relieved from his duties as discantist; but in consideration of his industry and good conduct, also of the unusual musical gifts with which nature had endowed him, he would continue to enjoy the privileges of free scholarship, and that he had suggested him to the leader of the choir as an assistant in the instruction of the younger pupils in music.

Who ever was happier than Sebastian? He fervently thanked the Rector for his kindness, reverently kissed his hand, and hastened away with a joyous heart.

One day his friend Erdmann, who had been on a visit to his father in Hamburg, returned and told him of his experiences. "Upon one occasion, a church festival, at which the renowned organist, Reinken, played, I wished with all my heart, dear Sebastian, that you were there."

"So you have heard him?" said Sebastian, excitedly.

"Yes, and for a whole hour. That was playing for you! I never have heard the like of it. Everyone was excited. Women wept."

"What did he play?" asked Sebastian, breathlessly and with his very soul in his eyes, as he looked at his friend.

"First a magnificent prelude[14] for full organ in E major, preceding an artistic fugued chorale of wonderful beauty ('We all believe in one God'), and at the close a fantasia on 'Jesus, my Joy.' Oh, if you only could have heard it, Sebastian! He can play much more beautifully and skilfully than Böhm."

Sebastian was completely self-absorbed. "I must

[14]An introduction to a chorale or fugue, and sometimes, as organists frequently improvise on a chorale, a free fantasie. A fugue is generally preceded by a prelude which stands in the same key.

hear him," he said at last, fixing his gaze upon his friend. "I must, I must, even if I have to give up everything here."

"That is not at all necessary," quietly replied the less impulsive Erdmann. "If you apply in the regular way they will give you leave of absence for Sunday and Monday. Then you can easily go to Hamburg on Saturday afternoon, which is your free time, and get back again on Monday after hearing Reinken."

"I will do it. Oh, I will do it, the very first thing to-morrow morning. God grant they may not refuse me permission; I will even go to extremes to secure it."

"Yes, yes, but don't dash your head against the wall," said Erdmann. "There is time enough for you to hear Reinken even if you do not go next Sunday. He will live to be a hundred years old."[15]

Sebastian did not hear his last words. So intense was his longing to go that he lost no time in asking permission from the leader of the choir, and finally obtained it with the aid of the Rector.

After dinner on Saturday he sped away with flying feet and began his long twenty-five miles' journey to Hamburg. He reached the city late in the day, very tired, hungry, and thirsty, but determined not to miss Reinken's playing early in the morning.

He found quarters for the night at a modest inn, but he slept restlessly. He awoke, however, refreshed, his fatigue having disappeared. He was prompt at the

---

[15]Reinken was born in 1623 and died in 1722. At this time he must have been about seventy-seven years of age.

early service, and found a seat among the first-comers to St. Katherine's Church, where he waited with fast-beating heart the first tones of the majestic instrument from the hands of the great master.

And now, now the first tone rose, like the first rays of dawn, undulating, palpitating, rising and falling, and then streaming out in a mighty tone-flood, vivifying and uplifting the hearts of the listeners. Truly it was the playing of the supreme master, the art of perfect organ-playing and great contrapuntal skill, the ideal which had so long filled the soul of this gifted boy. He determined to strive for like perfection with all his powers and with absolute devotion to the work. In that sacred place, where the highest revelations of art had been made clear to him, he vowed to himself he would never be satisfied with any lower standard, he would never be contented with any less degree of mastery of the sublime and exalted craft of music.

CHAPTER IV

THE NEW LIFE

AN unexpected opportunity being offered to hear the famous organist again after Sunday, Sebastian had no scruples against remaining a few days longer in Hamburg. He returned to Lüneburg on Wednesday in such a musical exaltation that he gave no thought to the possible consequences of his violation of duty. No reproaches, no penalties, however, could disturb him. He had secured treasures that forevermore elevated him above the petty, common things of life.

Though he had lived very economically during his prolonged stay in Hamburg, he had so far exhausted his little means that he began the return journey with only a few pfennigs in his pocket. Notwithstanding his youthful strength and endurance, he was soon well-nigh exhausted. Unable longer to endure the pangs of hunger, he stopped at an inn on the highway to ask for such food as his small means would purchase. A travelling carriage with four beautiful black horses was standing before the door. Inside there was lively commotion, for they were preparing breakfast for the distinguished travelling party. Sebastian stole quietly into the house and asked the inn-keeper, who was bustling about the coffee-room in a state of great excitement, for a herring (the favorite food of the poor in Thuringia) and a piece of bread, but no attention was paid to him. Puffed up with pride at serving such distinguished guests, he contemptuously ignored the young traveller, and when the request was repeated, refused it and turned him away hungry from the door.

Sebastian was so deeply grieved and hurt by this treatment he could hardly muster up courage to resume his tramp upon an empty stomach. His strength was well-nigh exhausted. He sat down on the turf before the door, half determined not to leave until the inn-keeper gave him food. He was sick at heart and discouraged. Suddenly a window was opened above him, and upon looking up he espied a kind-faced old gentleman, who threw a little parcel into the grass in front of him, accompanying the act with a cordial and significant nod of his head.

Sebastian was at first somewhat embarrassed. Then he picked up the little parcel, undid the fine white-paper wrapper, and two herrings and two nice little rolls dropped out. Deeply moved by the gift thus sent to him and casting a thankful glance at the window, he took out his pocket-knife and began to cut up one of the herrings. To his extreme surprise he found a Holland ducat in the fish. He took the second herring, and his surprise was increased when he found another. Perplexed and greatly agitated, he again gratefully gazed up at the window, where his kind benefactor significantly shook

Sebastian's Unknown Benefactor

his powdered head and then disappeared behind the curtains. Strengthened afresh by the herrings and rolls and encouraged by this pleasant incident on the last day of his long march, the happy boy set out again; but he saved his ducats for the next repetition of his musical pilgrimage to Hamburg.

His offence was expiated by a slight restriction of his privileges, but it in no way affected the goodwill or respect of his teachers. They regarded the liberty he had taken as a concession which was due to his genius, and continued to allow him the free school privileges in consideration of his industry and scholarly gifts. They realized already his great future.

During his three years' stay in Lüneburg, Sebastian by resistless determination and tireless industry rose step by step in all his studies as well as in his musical education, secured the requisite certificate for the University, and the highest recognition as violinist, organist, cembalist,[16] and contrapuntist,[17] and as a youth of exemplary character. Hence there was no question of his fitness for the position which was now offered him through the influence of some of his

---

[16]Clavicembalo was the name of the usual form of the piano in the sixteenth century. It was the successor of the clavichord and the predecessor of the hammer-clavier. It had various forms and names. In Germany it was called klavier and sometimes monocordo, and in England spinet or virginal, according to its size or shape. Cembalist is the equivalent of our word "pianist."

[17]In its general sense, counterpoint is the art of combining melodies. It is divided into two classes—plain and double.

Thuringian friends, that of violinist in the ducal chapel at Weimar.[18]

It was not without deep emotion that he left the old school, the good Rector, the leader of the choir, and his classmates and friends. He bade Erdmann's kindly uncle a cordial farewell and left an affectionate letter for Erdmann himself, who had quit Lüneburg and gone into business with his father, urging him to correspond with him. On a cloudy spring morning of 1703 the seventeen-year-old lad, head and heart full of highest resolutions and aspirations, passed through the gates of Lüneburg on his way to his new duties.

It seemed to Sebastian, who had never concealed nor lost his love for the Thuringian land, that in going to Weimar he was going home, and it was with a genuine home feeling that he regarded his modest little room with its outlook over garden and field to the far mountain lines of the Thuringian forest. He made himself at home there at once with his violin and music, and entered upon the duties of his position without delay. They were simple enough for one who had gained perfect facility by three years of tireless practice, but they were far from satisfying his ambition; for the Court had no higher ambition than to keep up

---

[18]Spitta, in his *Life of Bach*, says: "In former times Bach's grandfather had had an appointment at the court of Duke Wilhelm IV at Weimar. This, however, can hardly have been the cause of his grandson's being invited to the same town. Other ties must have existed of which we know nothing, but which of course would easily have been formed at Eisenach or Arnstadt." Bitter, in his *Life*, says Bach probably owed the appointment to his numerous relatives in the Saxon state.

a certain musical state with which he had no sympathy. He compensated himself for his part in this superficial "kling-klang" by arranging with the old cathedral organist to play for a pittance. On such occasions he gave full expression to his feelings and conceptions upon the powerful instrument, after the manner of Böhm and Reinken, and lifted the souls of those who listened breathlessly to his wonderful playing above all earthly things. It seemed as if the Reformation spirit inspired those tones, so full of religious exaltation, and stirred the dingy portraits of Luther, Melanchthon, and Johann Friedrich.

The recognition of Sebastian's success was not confined to Weimar and its people. It spread throughout Thuringia, and the "Duke's young violinist" had scarcely been in service six months before he was invited by the Schwartzburg Consistory to take the position of organist at the "New Church" at Arnstadt, formerly known as St. Boniface Church. He was greatly moved by the invitation. The old city of Arnstadt had been the home of Bachs for many generations. There his great-uncle Heinrich had lived and labored, as well as his father's twin-brother Johann Christoph, who so strikingly resembled him that it seemed to Sebastian he was now following in his dear father's steps. How could such an invitation help making him happy?

There was another thing that induced him to accept this invitation. The "New Church" was built upon the site of the St. Boniface Church, which was destroyed by fire in 1581, and was dedicated to divine service in 1683. The beautiful church had been without an organ twenty years, but one had now been secured by contributions. The well-known organ-builder, Johann Friedrich Wender, of Mühlhausen, had constructed an excellent instrument, and this was to be placed in charge of Johann Sebastian.[19] Joyously he exulted at the prospect of releasing its magical tones for the first time. He accepted the position with a thousand thanks, notwithstanding the small salary.

To add to his delight, several of his dear relatives lived in Arnstadt. The situation and environs of the place also were beautiful, and especially charming to one of Sebastian's cheerful disposition. As this was ample equivalent for the smallness of his income, he accepted the annual salary of eighty thalers, and went to Arnstadt.

The slight demands which his position made upon his time, left him leisure for the study of the German and Old French contrapuntists. He labored over their works most assiduously, to gain a more thorough knowledge of the comprehensive rules of the higher organ style. The better to express his own conceptions, he also arranged some new violin concertos of Vivaldi[20] for the piano, by which he gained a clearer understanding of the relations of musical ideas to each other and of the sequence of modulations. What he wrote down

[19]This organ was in use until 1863, when a fine new one took its place as a memorial to Bach.

[20]Antonio Vivaldi, a distinguished violinist and composer, was born at Venice and died as director of the Conservatorio della Pietà in that city in 1743. His works are very highly esteemed.

during the day without an instrument, he played over upon his piano in the evening and sometimes late into the night, until he had completely mastered the technic.

Beside all this, he assisted in the compilation of the Freilighausen hymn-book, and for the purpose of making the chorales more effective, he undertook the arduous work of rearranging three hundred of them and composing many new ones himself. His organ-playing was so rich and fanciful in his own conceptions that the congregation, accustomed as it was to exceedingly simple hymn-accompaniments, could not follow him, and this led to repeated complaints from the Consistory. Sebastian, however, striving only for the highest in his art, paid little attention to them. He only labored all the harder to perfect himself, ignored all practical matters, and gave heed to no authority above him when it interfered with the lofty purpose he had in view.

He found recreation after the fatigue of studies, composition, and practice upon the violin, piano, and organ, in the enjoyment of nature and in the society of relatives and friends. Among the former those most dear to him were the family of Johann Michael, Heinrich's son, a quiet, music-loving circle, the central attraction of which was the lovely, blooming daughter, Maria Barbara, Sebastian's studious and gifted pupil. Among his friends those nearest to him were Christoph Uthe, the minister of the "New Church," and Johannes Laurentius Stauber, assistant minister, both well-grounded in the higher church music and entertaining the utmost respect for Johann Sebastian's courageous struggle and energetic will. In this circle the young artist was particularly happy. There all the real worth of his unpretentious life was displayed. There he found warm appreciation for the highest and best, and never failing help and sympathy.

One evening he rushed into the Bach home, where both friends were visiting, and as if in utter despair flung himself down into a chair without a word of greeting. All looked at him with great concern. "Dear Bach," said Laurentius Stauber, solicitously, "why do you come rushing in in this unceremonious manner? Has anything unfortunate happened?"

"I am the unfortunate myself," exclaimed Sebastian, passionately. "I am a bungler, and I shall always be a bungler if I stay here. I am going away."

"Away from here!" they all exclaimed. "Where are you going?"

"Where there is something to be learned. I am going backward here. Soon I shall know nothing."

"But, Sebastian—" said Johann Michael, reproachfully.

"But it is true," he replied, gloomily. "My organ-playing is going backward. It has no depth, no vigor, no progressiveness—"

"But, dear Bach—"

"I tell you it is true, I feel it. My compositions also have no ideas. They show no charm of fancy, no mastery of materials. This cannot go on any longer."

"But you greatly underestimate yourself, cousin,"

said Johann Ernst, son of the twin brother of Sebastian's father. "Would to God I could play as well as you do already at twenty! Everyone here is astonished at your work."

"But what do they know about music here?" replied Sebastian, contemptuously.

"But we are astonished also," interposed Herr Uthe, "and we think we know a little something about sacred music."

"To be sure you do," said Sebastian, "but your friendship for me makes you blind. You do not see my failings. No, no, I must be off. I must hear once more the great masters of the art and find out from them how to get on the right road again. I am going away at once."

"Where will you go? Where will you find what you are longing for?"

"Where? Yes, that is the question," said Sebastian, with a sad look in his eyes. "Really there are only two places where I expect to find what I need—in Nuremberg with Pachelbel,[21] or in Lübeck with Buxtehude."[22]

"Both are certainly far enough away from here," said Herr Uthe, dolefully.

[21] Johann Pachelbel, a distinguished organist and one of the foremost promoters of the organ style before Bach, was born at Nuremberg in 1653 and died there in 1706 as organist of St. Sebastian's Church.

[22] Dietrich Buxtehude, born at Helsingør in 1637, was organist in 1668 at the Marien Church, Lübeck, and remained in that position until he died, May 9, 1707. He was one of the most learned organists and composers of the seventeenth century, but most of his works have been lost.

"What matters distance?" answered Sebastian, with some warmth. "I would go to the ends of the earth if I could hear the great organists there. But, to cut matters short, I shall go to Lübeck in the morning."

"Without permission?" asked Johann Ernst, very seriously.

"I am going to see the Superintendent this evening."

"And at this unpleasant season of the year? Think of that," said Johann Michael.

"A journey of at least sixty miles," added Herr Stauber.

"Let him go," suddenly said the soft, gentle voice of the one who alone of all the circle favored his plan. "He must do what his genius bids him do."

Surprised and greatly excited, Sebastian turned to the speaker, his young cousin Maria Barbara,[23] and thankfully offered his hand. "You understand me," he said with emotion; "now nothing more can restrain me." With this closing word he left the house.

Week after week passed. He had far exceeded his one month's leave of absence and nothing had been seen or heard of him. His friends were solicitous, his superiors indignant, the congregation angry. How could he so thoughtlessly violate his duties? What could he be doing? Where could he be? His conduct was

---

[23]Maria Barbara was the youngest daughter of Johann Michael Bach. She was at this time about twenty years of age and was a good musician. It is somewhat singular that in the numerous family of Bachs, Sebastian was the only one who took a Bach to wife.

simply incomprehensible to everyone. Maria Barbara smilingly shook her knowing little head when she heard the reproaches of relatives and friends, the slurs of neighbors, and the threats of the Superintendent, and said: "You are wasting your words. Sebastian would not care if you should even say them to his face. He is living and working for higher things than those which are deemed of so much importance in Arnstadt."

And so it turned out. Two, three months passed, and the indignation of the church-wardens was at its height, when one fine day Sebastian suddenly appeared at Johann Michael's and cheerfully greeted his astonished relatives. He replied coolly and unconcernedly to the storm of exclamations, reproaches, and questions, tenderly greeted his pretty little cousin, Maria Barbara, and at last, when questions and complaints had ceased, said briefly, "I am accountable for all that I have done or may do. My journey to Lübeck was made solely in the interests of the art which I practise for the honor of God and for the edification of the Christian congregation. All other considerations must be subordinate to this higher purpose. Will the Consistory and Council of Arnstadt complain because in striving to rise higher and higher in my art I have exceeded the time allowed me? Possibly they may discharge me from my position. What does that matter? Arnstadt is not the world. At all times and in all places the world's door stands open for the skilful artist. Offers have already been made to me in Lübeck. So do not be troubled about me; I do what I must do and others may do what they please—so enough of this."

"I told you so," exultantly declared Maria Barbara, looking round the circle. "He cares not a whit for your anxiety about him. He will excel you all."

"Ah! you rogue," said Sebastian, smiling, "I did not know you were a prophet." The girl blushed to the tips of her ears as he bent over her and tenderly whispered, "Can you also prophesy the name of Sebastian's wife a year from to-day?"

"Oh! yes," replied Maria Barbara, "Frau Bach. She certainly will have that name."

"Oh, you cunning one! But the Christian name, the Christian name—that is the question. Well?"

"I cannot prophesy so much in one day," replied the blushing girl; "I will tell you that some other time."

"I will tell you to-day," whispered Sebastian. "She will be called Maria Barbara Bach. She is a dear, fair-haired maiden, and the only person who knows Sebastian through and through."

"Do not be too sure," replied Maria Barbara, in some confusion. "Sometimes my prophecies do not come true." The next instant she had slipped away and disappeared in an adjacent room.

"A year from now," the young artist said to himself, with all the solemnity of a vow, as his eyes followed her.

The apprehensions of his friends that measures would be taken by his superiors to call him to account were confirmed. He was summoned before the Consistory and sharply reproved for his audacious violation of his duties. His reply shows clearly his real purpose: "He had prolonged his visit to Lübeck solely in the interests of his art and for his own improvement, so that he might come back enriched with experience and many new ideas, which would better fit him for his position; and likewise he thought it would be better for his pupils. Beside this, he had provided a substitute for the organ."

This brief explanation of his conduct did not satisfy the old stiff-necked superiors, who did not at all understand him. Beside this, the simple members of the congregation, who did not appreciate his efforts to elevate church music, complained that he introduced strange variations in the chorales which they could not follow. This called for further explanation; rather than make which, Sebastian decided to resign his Arnstadt position and look for another.

Just at this time, Johann George Ahle, the highly esteemed organist at St. Blasius's Church in the old Thuringian imperial city of Mühlhausen, died, and the position was offered to Sebastian. He was ready at once, attended the organ examination, and so highly impressed the wardens with his playing, that they gave him the place. He expressed his satisfaction with the salary, requested and obtained his release from the Council at Arnstadt, and to his great delight found that his place would be filled by his cousin, Johann Ernst. To make the latter's position easy at the outset, for he was very poor, and beside had an old mother and sick sister to support, Sebastian gave up a considerable part of his back salary for Johann's benefit. Then he asked for the hand of his loving cousin, received her joyful consent as well as that of her family, and on a wonderfully beautiful, quiet, sunny Autumn morning went to Dornheim, where his faithful friend, Johannes Laurentius Stauber, was settled as minister. In the modest little village church, before the altar hung with festive garlands, the young pair exchanged rings and vows of love, and then, after a quiet, happy day spent in the parsonage, returned to Sebastian's own simple abode.[24] A few weeks later the happy couple settled in Mühlhausen and joyfully took possession of the organist's old house. The simple furniture, which they had jointly contributed, was soon cosily and comfortably arranged, and when everything was in its place and evening had come, the young bride-groom seated himself at the little piano, and with a heart overflowing with happiness sang and played the beautiful chorale:

> "I come, O Lord, before Thy throne
> This happy evening tide,
> And pray Thee, thro' Thy precious Son,
> Thou wilt with us abide.

[24]The following notice was inserted by Stauber himself in the parish register:

"On October 17, 1707, the respectable Herr Johann Sebastian Bach, a bachelor and organist to the church of St. Blasius at Mühlhausen, the surviving lawful son of the late most respectable Herr Ambrosius Bach, the famous town-organist and musician of Eisenach, was married to the virtuous maiden, Maria Barbara Bach, the youngest surviving daughter of the late very respectable and famous artist, Herr Johann Michael Bach, organist at Gehren; here in our house of God, by the favor of our gracious ruler, after the banns had been read in Arnstadt."

The Evening Chorale in the New Home

Accept this offering of the heart
Which now I humbly bring,
And of Thy grace to us impart
While I Thy praises sing." [25]

At the very first tones of the chorale, Maria Barbara stepped behind his seat and with clear and lovely alto voice joined in his sacred song. It was the consecration of the day, a beautiful beginning of the new life which God had prepared for them.

[25] In the original:

> "Jetzt komm ich, Herr, vor Deinen Thron
> Mit loberfülltem Munde,
> Und danke Dir durch Deinen Sohn
> In dieser Abendstunde.
> Nimm an das Opfer, das ich Dir
> Mit meinen Lippen bringe,
> Und höre gnädig was ich Dir
> Zu Deiner Ehre singe."

CHAPTER V

A MUSICAL TOURNAMENT

SEBASTIAN entered upon the duties of his position at Mühlhausen with great enthusiasm, and the friendly assurances of the wardens as well as of the congregation seemed to promise a long and successful tenure of his position. This, however, could not be certain if anything stood in the way of the elevation and improvement of church music, which was the very end and aim of his life. It was impossible for him to adhere to the musty traditions and stereotyped usages of musical craftsmen in small towns. It was not only his purpose, but it was a necessity for him to produce new creations, exhibiting a richer abundance of ideas in enlarged form, and compositions which would spiritually uplift his hearers and inspire them with fresh religious exaltation. If this could not be done in Mühlhausen—and he found only too soon that it could not—then his stay there must be short. His effort to reform church music was at first obstructed, then openly opposed. The families of the early organists and their friends, who regarded the policy of the young man, "the very young man," as an insult to his predecessors, were grieved. Malevolent

51

townspeople criticised him, and gossiped among themselves to this effect: "The organist is a freethinker and a subverter. He has no respect for old and honored things. He devises innovations, and plays a frivolous, ornamental music instead of the plain, devout music which simple people can understand. Herr Ahle and his predecessors were a different kind of men. Perhaps they did not know as much as Herr Bach, but they were more pleasing organists in the sight of God." It was a pitiable condition of things for Sebastian.

Sebastian resolved he would endure this misunderstanding and malice no longer. With an impatient shrug of his shoulders he announced to his devoted young wife, "We must take up the staff anew, darling. We cannot grow in this atmosphere. I cannot live where I cannot work for my highest purpose; I must look around for another position."

"Do so, dearest," said Maria Barbara, smoothing his wrinkled brow with loving hand. "The world is large, and a musician of your ability will be everywhere welcome."

In like manner his decision was approved by his two gifted scholars in Mühlhausen, Johann Martin Schubart and Johann Kaspar Vogler, and by his real friends who had sympathized with his work during his short stay, and this confirmed him in making his decision final.

"I am going to Weimar in the morning," he said with the utmost composure. "The new Duke is a warm friend of music and loves the higher church style. Perhaps he will hear me and invite me to enter his service."

"If he hears you, he cannot help inviting you," said Maria Barbara, confidently. "God go with you."

He went—and behold Maria Barbara once more proved herself a true prophet. The musical circles of Weimar were delighted not only with his splendid playing upon the organ of the castle church, but also with his fine piano-playing. The impression produced by his performances was so convincing that the Duke at once offered him the position of court organist with a handsome salary, contingent upon his securing release from his post at Mühlhausen. Sebastian returned home delighted with his prospects, and great was the joy of all when he told them of the pleasant outcome of his Weimar visit.

"If I can get my release from here, we will settle down in Weimar this summer. What do you think of that, dearest?"

"Of course we will," replied Maria Barbara, most emphatically. "The blind fools here, who do not understand you, will let you go very willingly."

"And we will go with you," exclaimed his two scholars, Schubart and Vogler. "Need we stay here without you, master?"

"Of course not," said Sebastian, much pleased, and Maria Barbara added, "We will all stay together until you become masters."

"Which will take a long time," muttered Vogler.

The Mühlhausen Council, as was expected, found little difficulty in releasing the organist from his duties, and the happy pair and his two faithful scholars packed their little possessions in readiness for settling down in the Ilm city.[26]

"It is time for me to have rest and peace for a few years," said Sebastian, as he sat down to his desk after the change, "for here I expect, if God so wills it, to remain and take such firm root that at last I may produce the perfect fruit. Hitherto I have been only a little tree in a nursery, which the gardener has set out among others, or stuck into the ground for a week or so to save it, if possible, from dying. Here there is good soil. I shall grow strong and deep and do good work."

His expectations were gratified. Nine beautiful and profitable years were spent in his favorite Weimar—nine years of perfect domestic happiness, and of satisfactory musical activity and production and universally honorable recognition. It was there Sebastian laid the firm foundation of his later world-fame. It was there that he wrote those first compositions which revealed him as the creator of a new style, destined to elevate music from a time-serving, mechanical craft to the position of an independent art. It was there that a large family of children blessed his home and eventually became accomplished musicians under his faithful guidance and instruction, his two scholars, Schubart and Vogler, succeeding him in the same position.

Some of the cantatas composed by him at Weimar are of incomparable majesty and beauty; for instance, the inspiring one in G minor, "Aus der Tiefe rufe ich,

[26]Weimar is on the Ilm.

Herr, zu Dir" ("Out of the Depths have I cried to Thee, O Lord"); the wonderful one in E flat major, "Gottes Zeit is die allerbeste Zeit" ("God's own Time is the best Time of all")—well known under the name of "Actus Tragicus"; and the heart-stirring one, "Ich hatte viel Bekümmernis" ("My Spirit was in Heaviness"). These, with the one beginning with the symphony in C minor and closing with a wonderfully charming chorus in C major, comprise a brilliant group.

These and similar compositions, the like of which had not been known before, his unequalled organ and piano playing, and his extraordinary facility in developing variations or fugues from a given theme, made him, though hardly thirty years of age, a musical authority far and near. People came long distances to hear him play on Sundays. Young and old musicians studied the revelations of genius in his compositions; and his Prince, proud of his distinguished castle organist, appointed him ducal concert and chapelmaster.[27]

Bach's rising fame as a composer, as well as pianist and organist, a few years later was the occasion of a significant and extremely interesting event. Among his celebrated foreign contemporaries was the French musician, Jean Louis Marchand, who was considered by his own countrymen an unrivalled organ and piano player. In reality he was a vain, pretentious person, and much more conceited about himself than his uncritical and enthusiastic worshippers. The foolish fellow indeed was so arrogant in his manners that he offended the

[27]This appointment was made in 1714.

King of France, whose court organist he was, and was banished.

The supercilious musician was in no wise humbled by this bitter lesson, and his experiences during his travels in Italy and Germany were not calculated to make him less conceited. He was so successful in dazzling the music-loving public with the brilliancy of his compositions, as well as with the fascination and elegance of his playing, that he was everywhere hailed as a distinguished virtuoso and overwhelmed with applause.

Marchand at last arrived in Dresden, and appeared in a concert given at the Court of Friedrich August I, where the French taste prevailed at that time. The distinguished audience was so captivated by him that its applause was almost unlimited, and the King offered the arrogant Frenchman the position of chapelmaster with a very handsome salary.

To prevent the consummation of the King's offer, and at the same time to establish the superiority of German over French art, Volumier, the director of the royal orchestra at Dresden, who was well acquainted with Sebastian's great skill and knowledge, invited him to go to Dresden without delay, that he might expose the pretensions of this Frenchman and settle the superiority of German art, as well as the superior honesty of German character.

Bach, fully aware of the corrupting influence of French taste at that period, lost no time in accepting the invitation, and went at once to Dresden. Volumier, in the meantime, had commended him to the King and Queen as a musician of equal rank with Marchand, and he had barely arrived when a messenger from Court brought him an invitation to a royal concert, in which "the highly renowned French concert-master and unrivalled virtuoso, M. Jean Louis Marchand, will appear," containing also an intimation that the King would be glad to hear him play. He cheerfully accepted, and as he entered the hall in his plain black coat, accompanied by Volumier, whose face was glowing with anticipation, offered a striking contrast to the richly clad and decorated Court attendants. All eyes were fixed upon the simple Weimar organist, especially those of the Frenchman, who, dressed in silk, velvet, and point-lace, and blazing with gold and jewels, stared contemptuously at his simple but deeply earnest German rival.

The concert at last began. Marchand with a haughty smile, as if assured of victory, rose and went to the piano. He played the melody of a French song in a neat and spirited manner, varied it with many little artifices and refinements, and then, coming back to the melody, closed in spirited and effective style. A storm of applause greeted him as he rose. He looked around him with an air of triumph.

"Very artistic work," said Sebastian, as the courtiers and musicians crowded round Marchand, "and very elegantly and charmingly played."

"That is true," replied some of Marchand's friends,

with much satisfaction. "Surely he is the leading piano virtuoso of our time."

Sebastian was silent, and appeared to be thinking of the music he had just heard, when a page brought him an invitation from the King to play something.

"If Your Majesty will deign to lend a gracious ear to my humble playing," said Bach, modestly, "I am ready." He seated himself at the piano, and after extemporizing a little in his own masterful way, played Marchand's song through in most graceful style, and then varied it twelve times, each variation displaying originality and constantly increasing skill and musical scholarship. His auditors, even the connoisseurs, listened almost breathlessly. At last he brought his performance to a close with a bold and brilliant passage, rose from the instrument, and after a gracious bow to the sovereign went back quietly to his seat.

The silent astonishment of the assemblage now gave way to a veritable jubilee of applause, and the King, Queen, and Crown Prince were as enthusiastic as the rest. The arrogant but now thoroughly humiliated Frenchman, with rage and hatred in his heart, retired among the crowd and quietly disappeared.

On the morning following the exciting event Marchand received a very courteous letter from Bach, in which, after complimenting him upon his charming and elegant playing, he invited him to select any theme he pleased for variation by the former upon the piano in public, and expressed the hope that Marchand would likewise take one selected by him. The latter replied, accepting the challenge to this musical tournament.

Great preparations were made for the event, under the patronage of the Court. Friedrich August, who anticipated an interesting evening, owing to the rivalry of the two brilliant musicians, after receiving Marchand's acceptance, selected the great salon of his cabinet minister, Field Marshal Count von Flemming, as the scene of the tournament. The entire Court assembled at the appointed hour. All the leading musicians of Dresden were there. Volumier, cheerful in his confidence of victory, and Bach, quiet and serious as was his wont, came in after the audience was assembled. At nine o'clock the royal pair entered, preceded by Court officials and accompanied by the Count and Countess Flemming. There was one person absent—Jean Louis Marchand!

It was unheard-of rudeness to keep the King and Queen waiting. The guests sat in painful suspense, watching the door for the entrance of the Frenchman; but they watched in vain. He did not come. Count Flemming was in despair at the ruin of the evening's pleasure. With the King's consent a courier was despatched to Marchand's residence, who returned with the disagreeable intelligence that the Frenchman had left Dresden, post-haste, early in the morning. The news fell like a bombshell in their midst. The King was angry, the Court excited, the German musicians quietly satisfied. Bach alone appeared unmoved and uninterested in the intelligence. It was a matter of course to him that whenever a contest between French music and German music was proposed, French music would run away.

One of the King's pages again approached Bach and said: "His Majesty desires to speak with you."

Sebastian quietly followed the boy. Standing before the royal pair, he bowed low to the King and lower still to the gentle Queen Ebahardine, and modestly awaited their pleasure. The King scanned the calm, earnest face of the young master, which had not a trace of the embarrassment usually shown by persons summoned before his Majesty, and with flashing eyes and much excitement said, "Your rival, Monsieur Marchand, has not come to measure his skill against yours. What do you think of his conduct?"

"I can only think there must have been very strong reasons for his non-appearance before Your Majesty."

"You do not think that he is afraid to enter the contest with you?"

"It would not be becoming for me to think so," replied Bach, with some hesitation. "Monsieur Marchand is a very accomplished musician and excellent player. I would not assume that he is unable to improvise on a given theme. He may have refused my challenge."

"You think and talk like an honorable man," replied the King. "But as Marchand, whatever may be his reasons, is not here, may we not have the pleasure of hearing the other contestant? Will you not give us a specimen of your skill in variations on some theme to be given you?"

"I shall be very glad to do so, Your Majesty."

The Musical Tournament

"Well, then," said Friedrich August, addressing the Queen, "will Your Majesty give Bach a theme?"

The noble Princess, not accustomed to have attention shown her by her usually indifferent consort, blushed slightly, but after a little reflection, said: "The year in which we live revives gracious memories of our venerated Doctor Martin Luther and his majestic hymn, 'Ein feste Burg ist unser Gott' ('A Strong Castle is our God'). Will you take that chorale for your theme?"

"With all my heart, Your Majesty," said Bach, with much emotion. "It is not very easy to follow in the steps of that great man, but I will try with God's help."

With deep feeling in his heart he went to the piano. As he rested his fingers upon the keyboard, they moved with the skill and inspiration of a higher world, and the great Reformation hymn rang through the salon with a fervor that uplifted and inspired the souls of all. A devout silence rested upon the assemblage. All eyes were fixed upon the plain, simple man, whose eyes looked upward in a spiritual ecstasy. All listened as if enchanted with the wonderful tones which the gifted master evoked from his instrument. Grander and more majestic still was the effect when he built a fugue upon the Luther hymn. It revealed the lowest depths of the tone-world. The wonderful structure of word and tone rose to the loftiest heights of religious faith; and when at last his hands rested and the last sound had died away, it seemed to the deeply-moved hearers that they had come back from a purer sphere into the atmosphere of this life, with ardent longings for the one they had left.

The King, who was worldly minded and long a stranger to religious faith, was nevertheless greatly moved. The Queen, who was devout of soul, was moved to tears. It was a moment in which all present were lifted above the emptiness of court and everyday life as they had never been before.

Rich with praise and fame, Bach returned to Weimar from the Royal Court, with its exciting life, its splendors and luxury, to the organist's little house, full of simple happiness, soul-rest, and heart-peace; and with him went the enduring recollection of the tears of the pious Queen and the warm words of gratitude she spoke to him, with pale cheeks and with the deepest emotion, from trembling lips. It was an event never to be forgotten.

CHAPTER VI

LIFE AND WORK IN LEIPZIG

SEBASTIAN'S stay in Weimar ended in the memorable year 1717. The congregation considered him an eminent organist. As the ducal chapelmaster he held a high social position. His Prince let no opportunity pass to express his appreciation of him. But his increasing family, and the growing difficulty of supporting them, made it imperative for him to secure a more remunerative position, and Maria Barbara, though with some regret, appreciated and accepted the situation.

While anxiously looking about him, Bach received a cordial invitation from the music-loving Prince Leopold of Anhalt-Cöthen to take the vacant position of court organist and chapelmaster in the capital city.[28] The news was joyfully received at home. As the salary was much larger than he had been getting, Bach could not hesitate about accepting the invitation, and so he resigned his position in Weimar, though not without regret. He was consoled, however, by the thought that

[28]Cöthen was at that time the capital of the Duchy of Anhalt-Cöthen, which was united to Anhalt-Dessau in 1853.

as he was bettering his circumstances his action would not be misinterpreted.

It was a still greater consolation to know that his place in Weimar would be filled by one who was competent and thoroughly trained. His accomplished scholar and friend, Johann Martin Schubart, who had been a member of the family for ten years and to whom he was closely attached, was to be his successor. So Sebastian and Maria Barbara quietly left the Ilm city, where they had lived so happily for nine years and where his work had been so successful, and went to their new home with bright hopes for the future. These hopes were mostly realized, and particularly in the improvement of their outward circumstances. His income relieved him from the serious anxieties which had troubled him in Weimar, and thus left him free to work and create. He also enjoyed the unusual appreciation of a music-loving Prince, who not only manifested the highest interest in his work, but bestowed upon him his personal friendship, an advantage of no small value in those days. He was no longer the son of the poor cantor of Eisenach, brought up as a duty by his relatives; no longer the orphan who was censured and lectured by church fathers for his innovations, but a man in the very flower of life, in the full enjoyment of his musical freedom and allowed to work out his ideas in his own way, and a greatly honored composer, whose acquaintance was eagerly sought by prominent people and whose friendship a noble Prince was proud to enjoy. How far he had exceeded the conventional limits of his position is shown by the fact that, when a son was born to him in

1718, the Prince, his brother, August Ludwig of Anhalt, Eleonora Wilhelmina, Duchess of Saxe-Weimar, Privy Councillor Von Zanthier, and the Baroness Von Nostiz, stood as sponsors at the christening.

Aided by these favoring circumstances, and particularly by the active sympathy of Prince Leopold, Sebastian, incited by his strong passion for creating, entered upon a new path—that of instrumental composition. It was there that he brought to its highest development that use of the polyphonic style on the organ which was peculiarly his own. In rapid succession he produced those great works for piano, and in chamber and orchestral music, which have been admired from that time to this, viz., the six so-called "Brandenburg Concertos,"[29] several suites,[30] a large number of sonatas[31] and duets, not a few compositions for piano alone, his two-part inventions,[32] and three-part

[29]So called because they are dedicated to the Margrave of Brandenburg.

[30]The suite was originally a succession of various national dances. The four most characteristic parts are the Allemande, Courante, Sarabande, and Gigue. Sometimes they also include the Gavotte, Passepied, Branle, Bourrée, and Minuet.

[31]The Sonata (sounding piece) originally was the general term for instrumental pieces, as opposed to Cantata (singing piece). The present form was definitely established by Haydn, Mozart, and Beethoven. Its parts are Allegro, Andante or Adagio, Minuet with trio or a Scherzo, and Rondo or Presto.

[32]Inventions, a term first used by Bach in the sense of impromptus. They were small pieces for the piano, written in two or three parts, each developing a single idea. ·

symphonies,[33] and, greater than all these, the first part of that masterly and unrivalled work which is known as the "Well Tempered Clavichord"—a creation of art which required twenty years for completion.[34]

Before this great work was completed, a cruel fate overtook the master—a blow which the loving pair little expected when they began the new life with such bright hopes. During a journey which Sebastian made with the Prince, who was accustomed to take the waters at Carlsbad, his wife was stricken with a sudden and fatal illness, and to the unspeakable grief of the children died in a few days. The mail-service in those days was so wretched and uncertain that letters, especially those sent to foreign countries, were frequently long delayed, so that Sebastian received no tidings of his affliction. Little dreaming of the terrible loss he had sustained,

[33]Symphony (with sound) is a large musical work for full orchestra, in the form of the sonata, with much fuller development of the single parts and richer development of true color in particular instruments.

[34]The title which Bach gave to this work is as follows:

"The Well Tempered Clavier, or Preludes and Fugues in all the Tones and Semi-tones, both with the major third or 'Ut, Re, Mi' and with the minor third or 'Re, Mi, Fa.' For the Use and Practice of Young Musicians who desire to learn, as well as for those who are already skilled in this study by way of amusement. Made and composed by Johann Sebastian Bach, Chapelmaster to the Grand Duke of Anhalt-Cöthen and Director of his Chamber Music. In the year 1722."

The first part of the "Well Tempered Clavier," or "Clavichord," as it is usually called, was written in 1722, probably during some of his journeys with Prince Leopold. The second part was finished in Leipzig about 1740.

he spent some time with the Prince at Carlsbad, but at last, unable longer to resist his longing for home, he returned, only to make the dreadful discovery that the wife whom he had left so well and happy was in her grave.

Only a strong, devout nature, like that of Bach's, and the consolations of sacred music could have enabled the bereaved husband to endure such an affliction. The sorrowing Sebastian nevertheless passed sad days, weeks, and months, and even the warm sympathy of the Prince had but little consolation for him. Fortunately, two important duties fully occupied his time—the education of his children and the musical instruction of his three gifted sons, Wilhelm Friedemann, Carl Philipp Emanuel, and Johann Gottfried Bernhard, which kept him absorbed in his art. A journey which he made about this time to Hamburg was also of great help to him. He went there to see, and, if possible, to hear, Johann Adam Reinken, the greatest master of the perfect organ style and of counterpoint, and bring back still higher standards for his own work. He was welcomed by the musical circles of Hamburg as a famous and honored master; but the old Reinken, being frail and weak, was inaccessible, and Bach soon began to grow uneasy at the possibility that he might have to return without gratifying his desire, when suddenly and unexpectedly a happy chance relieved his suspense.

On one of the last days of his stay in Hamburg, Bach played before a large and very distinguished audience upon the fine organ in St. Katharine's Church. When the applause had ceased and he was about to leave the organ, an earnest and unanimous request was sent to him to improvise upon a chorale, and he consented. He selected the chorale "By the Rivers of Babylon," which Reinken, at the very outset of his career, had arranged in a similar manner, and improvised with marvellous skill in long and artistic variations upon the noble theme.

His listeners were deeply moved by the breadth and power of his playing, but the player himself was still more deeply moved when the venerable Reinken, then in his ninety-ninth year, rose with effort from his seat in the front row, came forward and embraced him, saying with deep emotion: "I thought this art had died out; now that I see it still lives, I shall pass away in peace."

Bach was greatly affected by the occurrence and the master's parting words. No worldly recognition, not even that of the King, could have made him so happy. Tears came to his eyes, and he returned the old man's embrace with ardor and as if reluctant to let him go. Bach left Hamburg with a feeling of exaltation he had never experienced before. It seemed to him he was wearing an invisible crown.

The beautiful and powerful organs of Hamburg, as well as the many music-loving and musically intelligent circles of Handel's city, which had welcomed him and recognized his ability, were precious memories to Sebastian long after his return. How insignificant little Cöthen appeared in comparison! How lonely he was there with no opportunities to utilize his great skill and knowledge! Had it not been for the Prince, who fully appreciated his high purpose and loved and understood

"I thought this art was dead; now that I see it still lives
I shall pass away in peace."—REINKEN

music so well, and for the friendship he had bestowed upon him, Bach's craving for a higher sphere of activity, and his longing for better musical advantages and a more intelligent and appreciative musical public, would have induced him to look about for another field of labor. But there came a time, at last, when the sole consideration that kept him in Cöthen was removed in a singular manner, and he could justify his leaving.

The Prince, who had long been on most cordial terms with the court of Anhalt-Bernburg, was betrothed to a princess there, and became so absorbed in his approaching nuptials that his interest in music began to wane and his friendship for Bach became perceptibly weaker. Sebastian was greatly troubled about it, but he decided it was only fair to make some allowances for the Prince, and tried to believe that the old love (for music) would at last assert itself and take its place next the new love, and that the old friendly relations would be completely restored. In this hope he waited, but he was doomed to disappointment. There was a complete change in his princely patron and friend. His interest in music lessened more and more, and when at last the young Princess came, it was apparent that she had no real love of music. As Bach expressed it, she was simply bent upon being entertained, and henceforth music at Court would only be an amusement. This rendered Bach's position not only unprofitable, but absolutely useless, and thus the last tie that bound him to Cöthen was severed. He was now as eager to get away as formerly he had been eager to get there.

As if for the very purpose of providing him a place where he could find full scope for his ability, Kuhnau, the esteemed musical director of the St. Thomas School in Leipzig, died,[35] and Bach decided to apply for the position. The matter of filling the vacancy was deferred to the next year; but in the Summer of 1723 an invitation was sent to him and to two other fellow-workers in music to go to Leipzig and show proof of their skill. The decision of the judges was in Bach's favor after they heard his performance of his beautiful cantata, "Jesus called the Twelve unto Him." He entered upon his duties at once, and in this position he rose to the summit of his art. Death alone released him, a quarter of a century later.

The directorship of St. Thomas's was not unworthy of Bach. The traditions of the school were dignified, and its standing was high. He was at the same time musical director of the St. Nicholas and St. Thomas churches, likewise of St. Peter's and the "New Church." He was also leader of the "Alumneum," consisting of fifty or sixty "Alumni,"[36] who were obliged to assist in the church musical services. This school, which grew out of the convent of St. Thomas, had had many excellent teachers and had attained a high standard of excellence. Both patrons and teachers had striven earnestly to maintain this standard and also to keep the

[35]June 25, 1722.

[36]The "Alumni" were charity children, who were provided with food and lodging in the schoolhouse and a small allowance of money in consideration of their singing in church and at funerals.

musical department up to the high rank of the classical. Bach therefore undertook the task of maintaining old and time-honored traditions and standards. He ranked third among his colleagues, after the Rector, a head-master, and the co-rector, or assistant-master, and alternated with them in school inspection.

This comprehensive scheme of duties, and his general surroundings in Leipzig, had a powerful in-fluence upon the great musician. Famous as the city of Handel, and as a centre of life and movement, it was also a centre of great intellectual activity, and boasted among its educators men of European fame. Beside this, Leipzig enjoyed unusual freedom in the control of its municipal affairs, which gave the city a lively, flourishing aspect, all of which could not fail to make a deep and favorable impression upon a man of Bach's active, resolute disposition. In this vigorous atmosphere he revelled in the spirit of republican independence, and his passion for musical creation grew stronger, and remained strong to the end.

He was also delighted that at last he was able to carry out his plans with regard to organ work. He had at his disposal the so-called "greater organ"[37] of St. Thomas's Church, which had been there for two centuries and had been thoroughly repaired three years before this time. Bach was transported with delight as he awoke and set in motion the slumbering tone-forces of this

[37]There were two organs in St. Thomas's Church, a large and a small one. When Bach's great Passion music was given there, both were used.

magnificent instrument. It seemed to him there was nothing more to wish for in life.

The sorrow occasioned by the death of his faithful wife at last gave place to domestic happiness. For the sake of his children, who needed a mother's care, he married again, and in Anna Magdalena Wülkens,[38] daughter of a court musician to the Duke of Weissenfeld, he found a beautiful compensation for his loss. She transformed the sad house into a happy home. She brought up her stepchildren faithfully and carefully. She appreciated the great musical schemes of her husband, assisted him in his work, not only with all her heart's affection, but with much musical ability, took lessons from him, copied his manuscripts accurately, and sang in the choir,—for she possessed, greatly to Bach's delight, a fresh, young, beautiful soprano voice.

In the meantime the older children by the first marriage grew up strong and full of promise. The first-born son, Wilhelm Friedemann, was wonderfully precocious in his early youth. His father naturally was very fond of him, and had taught him with the utmost care. He was ambitious to leave to posterity a worthy successor, qualified to continue his own life-work, perhaps to surpass him. He had reason to believe this. Even in boyhood Friedemann had virtually mastered

---

[38]Anna Magdalena was the youngest daughter of the court-trumpeter, Johann Casper Wülkens. She was at this time twenty-one years of age. They were married December 3, 1721.

the piano and organ, performed the most difficult exercises in counterpoint with as much ease as if they were mere play, and "lived and moved" in music.

In general education, also, Friedemann was not behind any of his associates. In St. Thomas's School, which was very progressive, he advanced rapidly from one class to another, and also became an accomplished violin virtuoso under the instructions of concertmaster Graun, afterward chamber musician to Frederick the Great. He left the school at an early age, and studied at the University with the most famous teachers enthusiastically and successfully. From there he came home and entered the competition for the organist's position at St. Sophia's Church in Dresden. He was looked upon there as the favorite son and scholar of his great father. The dignity, grandeur, and power of his playing excited the astonishment even of the musical critics who heard him. His command of the instrument was so absolute, and his improvising so rich, new, and varied in style, that his hearers could hardly believe their ears, and many of them had trouble in following the flight of his genius.

After the trial, the judges unanimously agreed that Friedemann was by far the best and most skilful among the candidates, and so the youth of twenty-three was officially assigned the important place at Saint Sophia's Church. What joy and satisfaction filled his father's loving heart! It was one of the happiest days of his life!

Alas! he little thought that a demon was menacing the genius of the youth, a demon that would attack it incessantly, and ultimately destroy it.[39]

Next to Friedemann, and equal with him in his educational acquirements, was the highly gifted second son, Carl Philipp Emanuel. He was ten years of age when the Bach family left for Leipzig, but even then manifested such unusual musical promise that his father's fondest expectations were encouraged, and in this case they were fulfilled.

It is time to return to Bach, the father. It has already been said that his life and work were greatly influenced by his new residence and the change in his circumstances. It was in Leipzig he displayed those extraordinary achievements which were little understood by his contemporaries, but which have been admired for their beauty and regarded with astonishment for their scholarship by posterity. These great achievements were also accompanied by extraordinary wealth of production. Bach's creative energy at this time was like a rushing stream. No musician before or since has accomplished such results in composition as Bach during the Leipzig period. Music of every kind poured forth rapidly and in rich abundance. Oratorios and Passion music, cantatas and motets, masses and concertos, piano and other instrumental works, and, greatest of all, that priceless treasure of profoundly conceived and perfectly

[39]Wilhelm Friedemann was an accomplished musician, but in his later years he was addicted to drinking, which in time reduced him and his family to poverty, and eventually killed him.

constructed preludes and fugues, which the German people claim, and always will claim, as their own most beautiful and intellectual musical possession, are the outcome of the comparatively brief Leipzig period. How rich, deep, and varied were the creations of his intellect! How resistlessly he struggled on in spite of musical trademasters! How thoroughly he studied the works of the great masters of the past and of his time! He copied with his own hand a mass of music which was of use to him in his work, finished his masterpiece "The Well-Tempered Clavichord," instructed half a hundred Alumni, beside numerous private scholars and his own children, kept up a constantly growing correspondence, and read with absorbing interest everything in print at that time which had important bearings upon his work. Posterity can only wonder how the great master, in addition to all this, found time to look after his private affairs and those of his large household.[40]

[40]Bach had eight children, five sons and three daughters, by the first wife. The eldest daughter, Caroline Dorothea, born in 1708, survived her father. The eldest son, Wilhelm Friedemann, was born in 1710. Carl Philipp Emanuel, the most famous of the sons, was born in 1714. By the second wife he had thirteen children, seven of whom were sons. Only two of them survived their father—Johann Christoph Friedrich, born in 1732, died in 1795, and Johann Christian, born in 1735, died in 1782.

CHAPTER VII

"HE SHALL STAND BEFORE KINGS"

BESIDE the burdens of his official position and the fatigue of his extraordinary musical activity, Bach realized the infirmities of old age at a comparatively early period. He had overtaxed his strength in his youth, and this now began to affect his physical powers. He was also threatened with the loss of sight—a possibility which greatly alarmed his family.

On account of this danger, he exerted himself as rapidly as was judicious in preparing his children for their future work and fitting them to act for themselves. As has already been said, Friedemann, his most gifted and best-beloved son, had been organist at Dresden since 1733. Bach had often visited him, and sought by paternal counsel and affectionate warning to dissuade him from the eccentricities and extravagances to which he was prone, and to keep him in the right path.

The second son, Carl Philipp Emanuel, was very successful in the University, which he left in 1738, and proved himself not only such a gifted musician but excellent scholar in the sciences, that the Crown Prince of Prussia, known in history as Frederick the Great, summoned him from Rheinsberg to take the place of pianist in his musical chapel. There we shall shortly see him.

The third son, Johann Gottfried Bernhard, born at Weimar in 1715, was such a skilful player and accomplished contrapuntist at the age of twenty that he was fitted to fill an organist's position with credit. A position of this kind was offered him about this time, partly at the solicitation of his famous father. Mühlhausen, the city in which Bach himself, a quarter of a century before, had spent the golden days of his first youthful freedom and domestic happiness, in grateful remembrance of the famous father gave the not-yet-famous son the organist's position, much to the former's delight.

Not long after this, another occurrence gave Bach great satisfaction. The Elector of Saxony and King of Poland, Frederick Augustus III, who was so greatly interested in the musical tournament at Count Flemming's palace, when Marchand, the Frenchman, evaded Bach's challenge by flight, had not lost sight of the master. After hearing him play at a church concert in Dresden, he appointed him "composer to His Majesty the King of Poland and Elector of Saxony"—a distinction which at that time was much sought after because of its personal value and far-reaching influence.

The old saying, "A prophet is not without honor save in his own country," was verified in Bach's case. He was greatly annoyed and distressed by serious differences and often very disagreeable disputes with his superiors, and sometimes with the Rector, over the affairs of the Thomas School and Church. Those small souls could not understand, much less appreciate, the unequalled achievements of a musician like Bach. From their point of view he was simply the Cantor of St. Thomas's, and they grumbled and found fault whenever his actions or regulations were not in accordance with their common-place ideas. The continual vexation which this caused him, as well as the feeling that such conduct on the Rector's part must eventually bring both himself and his work into disgrace, led him seriously to contemplate resigning his position in Leipzig and seeking a new home elsewhere. With this contingency in view, he turned his eyes to Danzig, a music-loving city, and with all the more hopefulness because Erdmann, the old true friend of his boyhood, lived and held an important position there. Since their separation at Lüneburg, Bach had kept up an irregular but cordial correspondence with his friend, and had the satisfaction of knowing that he held him in affectionate remembrance, and sympathized warmly with him in his welfare as well as in his troubles. Bach stated his circumstances to him with the utmost frankness, and complained of his meagre salary and the restrictions placed upon him by his unappreciative superiors, which exposed him to continual annoyance, jealousy, and persecution. Erdmann, who held an imperial position at that time, was extremely cordial, and promised to use his powerful influence in carrying out his friend's wishes, though he could not do anything right away in securing a situation for him. This was not necessary, for relief soon came from another source.

That same year the rectorate was vacant, and, greatly to Bach's delight, the learned Professor Gesner,[41] who knew the value of his work, succeeded to the position. The change in his circumstances made the life of the greatly troubled and poorly paid Cantor much more endurable, both in Leipzig and in the school. To the close of his life he found consolation for all earthly trouble and insufficiency in those inexhaustible sources of lofty musical ideas which God had given him to develop to the highest point of which he was capable, and to hand down to posterity in unsurpassed form. His happy domestic life, the success of his children, and the fine progress of his scholars, who gradually became skilful musicians, also strengthened and encouraged him; while his intimate relations with the Thuringian members of the family, who often visited him, and admired and loved him, helped keep his heart young.

Thus the years passed,—years of continuous care and toil, of faithful work "for the honor of the Highest," of many severe personal trials, but also of many kindnesses, which strengthened the heart of the master as he grew aged. His fame grew beyond Leipzig. The number of his majestic tone-creations greatly increased.

---

[41]It was Professor Gesner who wrote in one of his works upon ancient music: "I, my Fabius, who am in other respects an admirer of antiquity, am of opinion that my Bach and others like him unite in their own persons many Orpheuses and twenty Arions."

He was without a rival as a profoundly learned composer and skilful organist and pianist. And yet with all his honor and fame he worked quietly, unpretentiously, and manfully in his little closet at home for the support of his large family, and with absolute sincerity devoted his work to the glory of the Highest.

The saddest burden of his last years was the growing misconduct of his favorite son, Wilhelm Friedemann. Even in his boyhood he had manifested abnormal tendencies toward eccentricity, and in the course of years it had made him more and more disliked. Beside this, still worse traits of character revealed themselves, such as imperious haughtiness and repulsing moroseness of disposition, persistent indulgence in extravagant and bizarre musical fancies, notwithstanding the warnings of his father and friends, and, finally, over-indulgence in drink. Owing to his insolence, he had to leave his position in Dresden. With much difficulty he secured the place of organist at St. Mary's Church, in Halle; but even there, desirable as the position was, he made no effort to curb his extravagances and dissolute habits, so that his father had good grounds for solicitude as to his future. And yet he charmed everyone with his fanciful and brilliant playing, and the hope was generally expressed that his talent would ultimately reach as high a standard of development as that of his father.

The progress of the second son, however, rejoiced the heart of the much-enduring old master. After the Crown Prince Frederick succeeded to the throne made vacant by the death of his father, Philipp Emanuel was appointed royal chamber musician and court pianist at Potsdam and Berlin, and was at this time enjoying the personal and musical distinction he so well deserved. Everything that came from him—letters, compositions, musical tidings of every kind—brought joy to the old father at St. Thomas's, and caused him to rejoice in the rising fame and good fortune of his manly son. A message which Emanuel sent at this time to his father made ample compensation for all the trials of the last few years, and filled the modest home at St. Thomas's with unalloyed satisfaction and delight. Frederick II, King of Prussia, the admired of all the world, victor at Hohenfriedberg and Sohr,[42] expressed his sincere admiration of "Master Bach" and the wish to see him in Potsdam as soon as convenient.

Bach was deeply moved by the message. All thoughts of his troubles in Leipzig disappeared, all his anxieties and cares were forgotten, and with fresh strength and courage he faced the future. There was nothing higher, nothing more precious in his estimation than his personal recognition by the greatest prince of his time. The future had nothing in store for him that could shake his courage or lessen his creative energy.

And yet the modest musician delayed gratifying the wish of the King. It was only when Frederick repeated

[42]Hohenfriedberg is a town in Silesia where Frederick the Great in 1745 defeated the Austrians and Saxons under Prince Charles of Lorraine. In the same year he defeated the Austrians at Sohr, in Bohemia; and 121 years later the Prussians defeated the Austrians at the same place.

his request in a more emphatic manner and threatened, in pleasant banter, to send a squad of hussars to Leipzig and arrest him and fetch him across the boundaries, that the old Cantor started for Berlin. With him went Wilhelm Friedemann, "Son of sorrow."

A tedious day's journey was coming to its close, and the Sunday vesper bells were ringing in the Potsdam turrets, when (May 4, 1747) our eagerly expectant travellers came to the gate, and announced their names and occupations to the gatekeeper, as was the custom. With anxious hearts they entered the city, and went to the quarter where Philipp Emanuel resided as court musician. Bach was received by his daughter-in-law most cordially, as was also Friedemann with sisterly kindness, and he embraced the grandchildren whom she brought to him at once, with much emotion.

"How delighted Emanuel will be," said the pretty little woman over and over, and then added significantly, "and also his Majesty, our all-gracious King. Scarcely a day has passed for a month, in which his Majesty has not asked at the evening concert, 'Is your father here yet?' or, 'When is your father coming?'"

"His Majesty is very kind," replied Bach, with evident pleasure. "We must announce our arrival without delay."

"The gatekeeper has done that already in his report, but it will also be well to send word to Emanuel before the evening concert begins. He has already been at the castle an hour, tuning a fine Silbermann piano."

Thereupon the brisk little woman went out and sent a boy-pupil with the message, bidding him go to the castle as fast as he could. The two travellers in the meantime refreshed themselves, after the fatigue of their journey, with a hearty meal, and were chatting cosily with Frau Gertrude, when the house-maid appeared at the door and announced a court messenger, who wished to speak at once with Herr Music Director Bach, of Leipzig. He was bidden to enter, and Bach greeted him with a pleasant smile, as if aware of the nature of his message. The messenger made a courtly bow, and said: "His Majesty has heard of the arrival of Herr Bach, and graciously orders him to appear without delay at his castle. I am ordered to accompany him."

"I will put on a more fitting dress," replied Bach, somewhat excited, "so that I may make as suitable an appearance as possible."

The messenger, however, promptly informed him that would be against his Majesty's express command. "I am ordered to fetch you to the castle without any delay."

"Well," said Bach, smiling, as he somewhat ruefully surveyed his homely but well-fitting brown coat, "the command of his Majesty must be obeyed. Let us go."

In the meantime there was a scene of exciting interest at the castle. At the hour appointed for the concert, the entire royal chapel was assembled in the music hall. It promised to be a notable evening, for the King was to play first flute in a concerto. The members of the chapel, among them Graun, Quantz, Agricola,[43] and Emanuel Bach, were engaged in earnest conversation about the piece, when a quick step was heard and the King entered.

The young sovereign carried a roll of music under his arm, and in his hand his favorite flute in its velvet case. With a genial smile and a hearty "Good-evening, gentlemen," he went to the piano, laid down his flute-case and began to arrange the music upon the desks, smiling at his players and saying in a bantering manner: "Well, gentlemen, we are going to try something of importance this evening. It is Quantz's latest work, and," turning to Quantz, "he has not made it very easy for us."

"Your Majesty," replied Quantz, with great respect, "music is not mere play for unpractised fingers and heads, but hard work."

"Yes, yes," replied the King; "I found that out while studying my part. I shall be surprised if we succeed in satisfying you."

---

[43] Karl Heinrich Graun was born at Wahrenbrück, Saxony, in 1701, and died in 1757. He was appointed chapelmaster when Frederick ascended the throne, and was also commissioned to organize a company of Italian opera singers in Berlin. He wrote operas for this company and several flute concertos for the King.

Johann Joachim Quantz, born January 30, 1697, died in 1773, was not only chamber musician and court composer, but Frederick's flute teacher.

Johann Friedrich Agricola, born January 4, 1720, died in 1774, was a pupil of Sebastian Bach and later of Quantz, and succeeded Graun in 1759 as director of the royal chapel.

"As far as Your Majesty is concerned, I am satisfied in advance."

"There! there! you are a flatterer. We shall see."

The King took his case from the piano and began putting his flute together. He was just about to try it, when the door opened and an official appeared, standing on the threshold and fixing his gaze upon the King.

"What is it?"

"If Your Majesty please, the gate-list."

"So, so; let me have it."

As the King, still with his flute in his hand, glanced over the paper, he suddenly gave a start, looked again, and turning to his band, said, "Gentlemen, great news! The elder Bach has come."

His announcement caused much excitement. Emanuel alone retained his composure.

The King's large blue eyes glistened, and smiles illumined his face. "Yes, yes, Herr Pianist, your eminent father has arrived, and undoubtedly this moment is at your residence. He must come here at once. I have waited to no purpose long enough. He must come at once—do you hear?"

"Is it Your Majesty's wish that I fetch my father?" said Emanuel, ready to start at once.

"Yes, yes, hurry!—or, no; stay here. There will be no end of questions and talk when you meet, and that means delay. I had better send another, who will bring him without any ceremony."

"Gentlemen, great news! The elder Bach has come."
—FREDERICK THE GREAT

The King rang a bell on the pier-table and a lackey appeared at the door. "Let a messenger be sent without an instant's delay to the residence of the court pianist, with instructions to fetch the organist, Herr Bach, who has just arrived from Leipzig, to the castle at once. Do you understand? The messenger must take no excuse of any kind for delay."

"As Your Majesty pleases."

The man disappeared, and the King turned to his band with a beaming smile. "We have the old man at last. Gather up your music, gentlemen; we will play your concerto, Quantz, some other time. This evening we shall listen to one greater than any of you."

The musicians obeyed, and then stood whispering together. All this time the King was pacing up and down the hall impatiently, with his flute still under his arm. At last he stopped. "Graun, a word with you."

Graun approached the King.

"Listen, Graun. We must let old Bach hear some good music of our own time. What have we to offer him from the opera repertory?"

"If Your Majesty please, we have Hasse's 'Artaxerxes,' Porpora's 'Annibale' and 'Mitridate,' Handel's 'Faramondo'—" [44]

---

[44] Johann Adolf Hasse was born near Hamburg in 1699, and began his career as a tenor singer. He wrote his first opera in 1723. In 1731 he was concertmaster of the Royal Opera at Dresden. His 'Artaxerxes' was produced in 1730. He wrote over one hundred operas. =>

"No, no! We must have something of our own."

"Perhaps one of Agricola's pieces."

"But, still better, why not one of Graun's?" said the King, laughing.

Graun bowed. "In that case, and in obedience to Your Majesty, I make bold to suggest the 'Galatea.'"

"Oh! because I myself stumbled around a little in that pastoral music?[45] Ah! ah! Graun, have you also begun to be a courtier? What will become of my band? No, no, we will not have 'Galatea.' We will have 'Demofoonte' or 'Caius Fabricius.' What do you think of those?"

"We have well practised both, Your Majesty, but 'Cinna' is completely ready. If Your Majesty is so disposed, we can give Herr Bach the first act of that."

"Good, good, we can manage it; but we will talk about it later. As to the rest, I wish—"

At that moment the door opened and the lackey announced, "Herr Bach, of Leipzig, is in the ante-room and at Your Majesty's service."

"Let him enter, let him enter," exclaimed the King,

Porpora was born in 1686 and died in 1766. He was a famous composer and singing teacher, and a rival of Handel in London.

Handel's 'Faramondo' was produced for the first time at King's Theatre, London, January 7, 1738. It was only given five times.

[45]Frederick assisted Graun in writing 'Galatea.'

as he laid aside his flute, and his face lit up with smiles. "Dear Bach, bring in your father."

Emanuel hastened to the anteroom, and a few seconds later father and son entered the hall together. With the most gracious friendliness and cordiality Frederick met the old master.

"I have you at last, my dear Bach," he said, affectionately offering both hands to him as he stood bowing low, "and now I propose to hold you fast. I have had hard work to get a sight at you."

The old, careworn master was deeply affected by his reception, and so agitated as he kissed the hand of the victorious sovereign that for a few minutes he was speechless. As soon as he could master his feelings, he expressed his profound gratitude for so much graciousness and kindness, explaining at the same time how difficult it was to get an extended leave of absence from his superiors.

"Well, we will see about that," replied the King, with a suggestive smile. "The deuce take those Leipzig fossils! They have made me also wait long and to no purpose for you. I will attend to this, and when I go to Leipzig again with my grenadiers—which I may do any time, as long as they keep that intriguing nuisance, Brühl,[46] in office—I will punish them in a way that will put an end to their nonsense."

[46]Count Heinrich von Brühl was a Saxon statesman under Augustus III. He became prime minister in 1747, and induced Augustus III to take sides against Prussia in the Seven Years' War.

The King then led the old master into the room and introduced him to the musicians at their desks, as well as to the gentlemen-in-waiting. He had a pleasant word for each, and showed so little embarrassment in his new surroundings that Philipp Emanuel was greatly surprised. The gentlemen of the Court also were favorably impressed by the old musician, who attracted them all by his simple dignity and ease of manner.

The King looked affectionately at him. "Dear Bach," he said with genuine tenderness, "I am doubly glad you arrived to-day. Only an hour ago two Silbermann pianos, for which I have long waited, were delivered at the castle, and I would like to have your expert opinion of them. I am aware that you are not an unconditional advocate of the Silbermann technic."

"I was not at the beginning," said Bach, modestly. "It would not have been right so long as its mechanism had serious faults; but in the course of years it has been improved by skilful and intelligent men, its faults have been corrected, and now it really is a masterpiece. Your Majesty has made no mistake in getting them."

"I hope not, I hope not," said the King; "but now let us look at them. One is in my workroom and the other is in my chamber. Ho, there! Lights! The gentlemen of the chapel are welcome to join us."

Headed by the King and Bach, they went from one room to another, and Bach tried seven of these pianos, extemporizing so delightfully that the King was lost in admiration. "Splendid! splendid! that was masterly, dear Bach!" he exclaimed several times.

"Your Majesty is too generous," said the old Cantor. "It does not require much musical ability to show off a piano. I pray you for some more important task than that."

"Well, well, if you call that of no importance we must try something else. Will you take a theme and construct a fugue and variations upon it?"

"Gladly, Your Majesty, and if you are willing I will use the piano in Your Majesty's workroom. It is the best of all the instruments."

"I think so, too. Come in, gentlemen."

All entered the apartment, eager with expectation, and grouped themselves around the piano. "Now, select a theme, dear Bach, and give us a three-part fugue, if it be not asking too much."

The old master smiled quietly. "Will not Your Majesty have the goodness to give me the theme?"

"What? I? And you will extemporize a fugue and variations at the same time?"

"If it so please Your Majesty, I will undertake it with God's help."

"Well, I must say—but you shall have your way."

The King went to the piano, stood a moment in thought, and then gracefully and elegantly played this charming theme:

"Does that satisfy you?"

Bach bowed respectfully, seated himself at the instrument, and began extemporizing a prelude of the same character as the theme, and as only he could do it. For some time he developed it beautifully, and then with graceful facility worked up the theme itself, in three parts, with such depth of feeling, richness of conception and harmonic color, and above all with such an absolute mastery of technic, that the musicians held their breath, and the King, standing behind Bach, was transfixed with astonishment.

"Marvellous!" he whispered more than once, and when Bach closed with a contrapuntal masterpiece, the so-called stretto,[47] he exclaimed enthusiastically: "Truly, there is but one Bach!" and embraced the deeply moved master with the affectionate familiarity of a fellow-artist. After this, he said he would retire to enjoy the impression made upon him, but would see Bach again the next day,

---

[47]"Stretto," as applied to fugues, means the following of response to subject at a closer interval of time than at first. The term is also applied to lively closing passages such as are found at the end of concerto movements and arias.

as he wished to show him the organs in the Potsdam churches and hear him play on them. Bach cheerfully consented, and after making his adieus passed a quiet evening in his own family circle.

The next day, at the appointed hour, the royal carriage stopped at Emanuel's door, and at the King's request Friedemann accompanied his father. They were soon at the Church of the Holy Spirit, where the organ was in readiness and the King was awaited. In the meantime the church rapidly filled up with persons of high social standing and Court attendants, and soon the King's carriage was heard at the door. With a quick step the sovereign entered, hastily greeting those in attendance, and making his way to the organ-loft, where he warmly greeted the master.

"Dear Bach, yesterday you served me a magnificent musical feast, which I greatly enjoyed; but you know the old saying: 'The appetite grows by what it feeds upon,' and I am free to say that to-day I am longing to hear a performance such as only you can give us."

"And what might that be, Your Majesty?"

"A fugue in six parts."

"Yes, but our theme of yesterday, as Your Majesty well knows, is not adapted to that style of polyphonic treatment. If Your Majesty will graciously choose one that is—"

"No, no, Bach, choose a fitting one yourself; we shall be the gainers thereby."

"Your Majesty has only to command."

The King nodded his assent, took a seat a little apart from his retinue, and Bach began.

A majestic prelude rang from the organ in a mighty flood of tone, ever bolder and more triumphant, until, reaching a climax, it gave place to the majestic chorale, "Ich weiss dass mein Erlöser lebt" ("I know that my Redeemer liveth"), which he developed in six parts with a dignity of style and a divine fervor that entranced his hearers. The characteristics of the theme and the accompanying modulations, the freedom and brilliancy of his treatment, the clearness of the composition, and the individuality of the single parts, all combined to make a marvellous performance. The King was so enthusiastic that he embraced the old master, and exclaimed with emotion: "I have heard the utmost of which the divine art is capable! I am glad I have lived to hear it."

It was an inspiring day for the great musician. His son, Friedemann, also had to play for the King when they came to another church, and was heartily appreciated by the musicians, who could not resist the charm of his talent and performance. Other days not less inspiring followed these. It was a time so full of spiritual comfort and contentment that Bach devoted himself to composition, and produced one great work after another as if he had renewed his youthful power.

The King paid him affectionate attention to the last day of his visit in Potsdam, showed him everything worth seeing and remembering in Berlin, and magnanimously tendered him the highest honors in the royal musical service, which, though with some heaviness of heart, Bach declined out of consideration for his son Emanuel, asking for himself only the continuation of the royal favor and kindness. With sincere emotion the noble sovereign promised this. Bach left Potsdam after many happy weeks, and returned to his disagreeable Leipzig post, with a melancholy presentiment that the King's promise to have another visit sometime would not be fulfilled.

CHAPTER VIII

THE LAST OF EARTH

IT was only natural for the old master, weighed down with official and other burdens in Leipzig, to recall the delightful days in Potsdam and live them over; but the recollection of them was not a mere idle, dreamy revery; all his deeper feelings were so engrossed with the realities of his art that he did not hesitate to respond to its exacting demands. He decided to reset the theme which the King had given him with all the skill of which he was capable. He completed the task in a few weeks. In its new form the work had thirteen numbers, finished with masterly ability. He engraved it upon copper and dedicated it to the King, with the title, "Musical Offering, humbly dedicated to His Majesty, King of Prussia." He sent it to the King with the following characteristic letter:

"All Gracious King:—Herewith I present to Your Majesty, with deepest respect, a musical offering, the noblest part of which is from your own hand. I recall with the highest pleasure the particular kingly grace with which, during my stay in Potsdam, Your Majesty condescended to give me a theme for a fugue on the piano, and to set me the task of working it out at once in your presence. As a subject, it was my duty to obey Your Majesty's command. I soon realized, however, that because of lack of necessary preparation, the execution was not up to the standard demanded by such a theme. I then determined, and at once set about it, to work out this royal theme more perfectly, and then give it to the world. I have done this to the extent of my ability, and with no other purpose than the exaltation, though only in one small particular, of the glory of a sovereign who must be admired by all in music, as well as in war and the arts of peace. I make bold to add the following respectful request,—that Your Majesty will deign to honor this small work by graciously accepting it, and continue Your Majesty's favor to Your Majesty's most loyal subject and obedient servant,

The Author.

"Leipzig, July 7, 1747."

While engaged upon this remarkable work, a new joy brightened his home. His daughter Frederica[48] was engaged to Altnikol, one of his best beloved scholars, who, upon Bach's warm commendation, was given the lucrative position of organist and musical director by the Council of Naumburg. This enabled them to marry and have a home, thus lifting another burden from the loving father. He could contemplate the evening of life with serene hope. His own were all provided for, and

[48]Elizabeth Juliana Frederica was born in 1726. Bach's first grandchild, the issue of this marriage, was named Johann Sebastian.

he now devoted himself with all his powers to a work he had long contemplated. The evening of life might end in darkness, but now he was ready to go before the throne of the All Highest, to whose service he had devoted his art piously and faithfully all his life.[49]

The great work which he had so much at heart was "Kunst der Fuge" ("The Art of Fugue"), a wonderful creation, unsurpassed in the abundance of its contents and their development. In completely elaborated numbers, not in dry theoretical rules, he shows what a skilful composer may accomplish with a single theme, and how it may be developed in the form and according to the rules of strict counterpoint in every possible way. So far as harmonious combinations are concerned, each part is exhaustively treated.[50] In the closing fugue, beside the two parts of the original theme, he introduces a short but very striking theme of only four notes; but those four notes represent the whole life of the composer, with all its joys and sorrows, its divine inspiration, and its deep soul-sadness—the four notes, "B-A-C-H." [51]

Bach's labor upon this colossal work exhausted what little strength he had. His eyesight began to fail.

[49]On all his important works Bach inscribed the initials, "S. D. G." ("Soli Deo Gloria"),—"To the glory of God alone."

[50]"The Art of Fugue" includes fifteen solos, two duets for piano in fugue form, and four canons, evolved from a single theme in two parts.

[51]"H" in German represents "B natural," "B" being reserved for "B flat."

His creative faculty was impaired. He could no longer work. The "Art of Fugue" remained unfinished. Philipp Emanuel added to the last bars of his father's manuscript the sad words:

"While engaged on this fugue, in which the name of 'Bach' is introduced in counterpoint, the author died."

It was true. The old master did not live to finish the work. The end was near at hand. Two operations were performed upon his eyes, but they failed to help him. His life passed into darkness before death.

But he never lost courage. His spiritual vision remained clear to the last, so that he beheld the glory of his God whom he was so soon to meet. In those last days, so full of pain and of sorrow over the thought that he might lose his faculties completely, he triumphed over sickness and death with the help of that lofty, unwavering faith which had been the inspiration of all his work. Almost with his dying voice he dictated to his beloved Altnikol the majestic chorale ("Wenn wir in höchsten Nöthen sind"):

> "When, sunk in deepest misery,
> To make escape we vainly try,
> When earthly help in vain is sought,
> And earthly counsels come to nought,
> There still remains this one relief—
> That Thou dost hear our cry of grief,
> And that our faithful trust in Thee
> From earthly ills will set us free." [52]

This trust, this deliverance did not fail him in those last days of pain and sorrow, in the last hard struggle. He rose triumphant over them, and the Almighty Father's hand led him to a place in the choir of angels and holy spirits who stand before the throne in adoration, singing, "Holy! Holy! is the Lord! Blessing, and glory, and wisdom, and thanksgiving, and honor, and power, and might be unto our God, forever and ever. Amen."

On the thirtieth of July, 1750, the world's greatest musician was buried in St. John's churchyard, Leipzig.[53]

[52]"By his deathbed stood his wife and daughters, his youngest son, Christian, his son-in-law, Altnikol, and his pupil, Müthel. He had been working with Altnikol only a few days before his death. An organ chorale, composed in a former time, was floating in his mind, ready as he was to die, and he wanted to complete and perfect it. He dictated and Altnikol wrote. 'Wenn wir in höchsten Nöthen sind' ('Lord, when we are in direst need') was the name he had originally given it; he now adapted the sentiment to another hymn and wrote above it 'Vor Deinen Thron tret ich hiermit' ('Before Thy throne with this I come')." Spitta's *Life of Bach*, Vol. III, p. 274.

[53]"In the church which for twenty-seven years Bach's mighty tones had so often filled, the preacher announced from the pulpit, 'The very worthy and venerable Herr Johann Sebastian Bach, court composer to His Kingly Majesty of Poland and Elector and Serene Highness of Saxony, chapelmaster to His Highness the Prince of Anhalt-Cöthen, and Cantor to the School of St. Thomas in town, having fallen calmly and blessedly asleep in God, his body has this day, according to Christian usage, been consigned to earth.' His grave was near the church, but when, within this century, the graveyard was removed farther from the church and the old site opened as a roadway, Bach's grave, with many others, was obliterated, and it is now no longer possible to determine the spot where his bones were laid to rest."—Spitta's *Life of Bach*, Vol. III, p. 275.

APPENDIX

The following is a chronological statement of the principal events in the life of Johann Sebastian Bach:

1685   Born at Eisenach, March 21.

1693   Began his studies with his brother, Johann Christoph.

1700   Chorister at the College of St. Michael's in Lüneburg.

1703   Organist of Arnstadt Church.

1707   Organist of St. Blasius's Church, Mühlhausen.

1707   Married Maria Barbara Bach.

1708   Court Organist at Weimar.

1720   Death of first wife.

1721   Married Anna Magdalena Wülkens.

1723   Cantor of St. Thomas's School, Leipzig.

1725   Composed first part of "Well-Tempered Clavichord."

1729   Composed St. Matthew Passion Music.

1734   Composed Mass in B minor.

1734   Composed the Christmas Oratorio.

1740   Composed second part of "Well-Tempered Clavichord."

1747   Dedicated "The Musical Offering" to Frederick the Great.

1749   Partly finished the "Art of Fugue."

1750   Died at Leipzig in his sixty-fifth year, July 28.